READ THEM ALOUD!

Can you recite for your friends any of America's great ballads?

Here's a book to help you entertain your guests, or hosts, add hilarity to a party or a picnic. It's a collector's item too, because this is the first time America's lusty, ribald, classic ballads have been put together in one book. You'll find in these delightful pages *Abdullah Bulbul Amir*, *The Man on The Flying Trapeze*, *Old Dan Tucker* and a hundred more!

Read them and roar with laughter, chuckle with glee, or shed a tear or two for legendary gals and guys long gone by. And remember: RECITE THEM ALOUD!

AMERICAN BALLADS — *Naughty Ribald and Classic*

A Premier Reprint

Compiled by Charles O'Brien Kennedy
with the assistance of David Jordan

A Premier Book

FAWCETT PUBLICATIONS, INC., NEW YORK

First RED SEAL printing, November 1952
Second PREMIER printing, August 1956

PREMIER BOOKS are published by
FAWCETT WORLD LIBRARY
67 West 44th Street, New York 36, New York

Printed in the United States of America

Acknowledgments with thanks—

Lothrop, Lee and Shepard Co., for permission to reprint "The House by the Side of the Road," from Dreams in Homespun by Sam Walter Foss.

Dodd Mead and Company, for permission to reprint "Johnny Appleseed" by William Henry Venable; "The Cremation of Sam McGee" and "The Shooting of Dan McGrew," by Robert W. Service.

Edward B. Marks Music Corp., for permission to reprint "My Mother Was a Lady" by Edward B. Marks and "In the Baggage Coach Ahead," by Gussie Davis. Copyright by Edward B. Marks Music Corp.

Duell, Sloan and Pearce, Inc., for permission to reprint "Lasca," from Songs of the Cattle Trail and Cow Camp by John A. Lomax. Copyright 1919, 1927, by John A. Lomax; 1950, by Ruby Terrill Lomax and Alan Lomax.

Dana Burnet, for permission to reprint "Sisters of the Cross of Shame." Copyright 1915, by Harper Brothers.

Helen Finger Leflar, for permission to reprint "Roy Bean," "The Dying Hobo," and "The Boston Burglar," from Frontier Ballads by Charles J. Finger.

Coward-McCann, Inc., for permission to reprint "The Ballad of Yukon Jake," by Edward E. Paramore, Jr. Copyright 1921, 1924, 1948, by Edward E. Paramore, Jr.

Appleton-Century-Crofts, Inc., for permission to reprint "Noah an' Jonah an' Cap'n John Smith" by Don Marquis. Copyright 1921, by D. Appleton & Company.

Duell, Sloan and Pearce, Inc., and King Features Syndicate, for permission to use "A Song of Panama" from Poems for Men by Damon Runyon.

Harold Van Doren, as legatee of Mrs. Mansfield's estate, for permission to reprint "The Eagle's Song" by Richard Mansfield.

Droke House, for permission to reprint "The Frozen Maid"; and "Maria Peripatetica" by Reginald Wright Kauffman, from Stag Lines.

Every effort has been made to find the original sources of material and the names of the authors of the ballads contained in this book. If we have omitted any credits or acknowledgments, we shall be glad to rectify such omissions in future editions.

To all ballad lovers—
Greetings!

For some fifty years now I have been a student and lover of ballads. I have tracked them down in library, schoolroom, village, and countryside, and I have listened to my good friends recite their favorites throughout the years. Always it has amazed me that there was no book devoted exclusively to the American ballad. Folk songs we have had, and folk tales—volumes of them—but the true American ballad has been tragically neglected.

Much of the history of our country, its people, manners, and customs, has been written in ballad form. The true ballad, of course, is a story in verse, usually handed down by word of mouth from generation to generation and generally by authors unknown. It is recited to groups in homes, in taverns, in clubs, by campfires—by modern counterparts of the ancient troubadours who went from village to village and sang their songs of brave deeds and brave men—their country's history. Many fine American ballads have been set to music, but music is not an essential of the art.

I was delighted when the editors of Gold Medal Books asked me if I would collect for them the first authentic book of the American ballad for their Red Seal edition—and I am pleased to have my labor of love reappear in this Premier reprint edition.

In assembling this anthology I have tried to present ballads the reader already knows and many he ought to know. While entertainment has been my aim, I am aware that entertainment has two functions: first, to play on the sensitive chords of the mind, and second, to titillate the muscles of the stomach. I admit, too, my own nostalgic tendencies, for who would not pass on to the future the treasures that brightened the past?

Many of these ballads have numerous versions, but every effort has been expended to obtain the originals. The authors of many are lost in antiquity, and such ballads bear the line "Unknown." A few will prove that what was serious yesterday may be laughable today. Others still retain their original mood. You will find that many of the pieces here are robust, salty, racy, of the soil. Well, that's the kind of country America is. That's how we grew.

You will find ballads that lightened the burdens of the hardy pioneers from Maine to California, singing of rocky soil, impenetrable forests, turbulent rivers, and uncrossed prairies. There are ballads of love and longing echoing out of lonely homesteads, deserts, and isolated mining camps. There are some that are nostalgic, such as the one in reverential memory of an obsolescent edifice that once stood near the woodpile in America's back yard.

There have been many ballads I have reluctantly omitted, as space is necessarily limited. There have been many included at the insistence of ballad-loving friends. I think that, all in all, we have here a collection that puts on permanent record and for the first time the ballad as known in the great tradition of America. Let me acknowledge the invaluable help of my friend David Jordan, a fellow member of The Lambs, whose energy and industry helped make this book possible.

CHARLES O'BRIEN KENNEDY

New York
1956

Take Your Choice....

To
Marie, Frank, Bill, and Richard,
ballad lovers all

JIM BLUDSO

by John Hay

Gone are the great days of the Mississippi sidewheelers and their hardy pilots, who raced their enormous craft till their boilers were ready to burst. Lincoln's young secretary John Hay, later to become Secretary of State under President William McKinley, authored this undying drama of one of the classic races along the father of waters.

Wal, no! I can't tell whar he lives,
    Because he don't live, you see;
Leastways, he's got out of the habit
    Of livin' like you and me.
Where have you been for the last three years
    That you haven't heard folks tell
How Jemmy Bludso passed in his checks,
    The night of the Prairie Belle?

He weren't no saint—them engineers
    Is all pretty much alike—
One wife in Natchez-under-the-Hill,
    And another one here in Pike.
A keerless man in his talk was Jim,
    And an awkward man in a row—
But he never funked, and he never lied;
    I reckon he never knowed how.

And this was all the religion he had—
    To treat his engines well;
Never be passed on the river;
    To mind the pilot's bell;
And if ever the Prairie Belle took fire,
    A thousand times he swore,
He'd hold her nozzle agin the bank
    Till the last soul got ashore.

All boats have their day on the Mississip,
    And her day come at last.
The Movastar was a better boat,
    But the Belle she wouldn't be passed;
And so come tearin' along that night—
    The oldest craft on the line,
With a nigger squat on her safety valve,
    And her furnace crammed, rosin and pine.

The fire burst out as she cleared the bar,
    And burnt a hole in the night,
And quick as a flash she turned, and made
    To that willer-bank on the right.
There was runnin' and cursin', but Jim yelled out
    Over the infernal roar,
"I'll hold her nozzle agin the bank
    Till the last galoot's ashore."

Through the hot black breath of the burnin' boat
    Jim Bludso's voice was heard,
And they all had trust in his cussedness,
    And knowed he would keep his word.
And, sure's you're born, they all got off
    Afore the smokestacks fell—
And Bludso's ghost went up alone
    In the smoke of the Prairie Belle.

He weren't no saint—but at jedgment
    I'd run my chance with Jim,
'Longside of some pious gentlemen
    That wouldn't shook hands with him.
He'd seen his duty, a dead-sure thing—
    And went for it thar and then:
And Christ ain't agoing to be too hard
    On a man that dies for men.

THE DYING HOBO

by Bob Hughes

All in an empty box car one cold and dreary day
Beside a railroad water tank, a dying hobo lay,
His chum he sat beside him with low and bended
    head,
And listened to the last sad words the dying
    hobo said.

"I'm headed now for far away where prospects
    are all bright,
Where cops don't hound a hobo, or pinch a man
    on sight,
Tell Brooklyn Jack and Murph and Jo just what
    I tell to you,
I've caught a fast train on the fly and now I'm
    going through.

"I'm going to a better land where brakies ain't
    so mean,
Where weiners grow on bushes and where dogs
    is never seen,
Where no one knows of rockpiles and when you
    wants a ride,
The Boss Con says asmilin', 'Pardner, won't you
    get inside?'

"Oh, pard, I hear the whistle, I must catch her
    on the fly,
It's my last ride—gimme a drink of whisky 'fore
    I die."
The hobo smiled. His head fell back, he'd sung
    his last refrain,
His pardner swiped his shirt and coat and
    hopped the eastbound train.

THE BOOTBLACK'S CHRISTMAS

by Barney Mullelly

Our forefathers, without the complications of modern life, were not afraid of the frankly sentimental. Tragedy in the old days was simple and understandable. A broken heart was just that, and tears were not idle tears. Here is one of the heartbreakers.

A bootblack slept in a dry-goods box, it was on a
    Christmas eve,
Tho' all alone in his scanty home in Santa Claus
    he did believe;
He slept on rags and straw, then placed his little
    shoes outside,
Just as he hung his stockings up before his mother
    died.
The night rolled on and no Santa came, but a
    thief crept soft and low,
As he stole away those little shoes that were left
    standing in the snow.

REFRAIN

Sad, sad, indeed, to see the lad standing in the
    storm alone,
Beside the empty dry-goods box that served him
    as a home;
And the look of disappointment—Santa Claus
    did him refuse,
But saddest of all was to hear him call Santa
    Claus bring back my shoes.

But a moment's time had scarcely passed till I
    was beside the lad.
What makes you weep, my dear boy? I said.
    Have you indeed not got a dad?
Oh, no, kind sir, he said, with a beseeching look
    to me.
My poor mother died a year ago, papa was lost
    at sea.
I started back when I heard this tale, for I was
    returning home.
Then I scanned his face, what did I trace? It was
    the outline of my own.
I grasped the box, as I held my child in a father's
    fond embrace.
I could feel that my brain was whirling and the
    hot tears rolled down my face.
On a whaleship I sailed for a six months' voyage
    to sea.
I was wrecked and cast on a foreign shore, where
    none could hear from me.
The truth was clear, my wife so dear, from earth
    had passed away.
I'd play'd the part with broken heart of Santa
    Claus that Christmas day.

REFRAIN

Thank God, indeed, to find my boy, although in
    the storm alone,
Beside the empty dry-goods box that served him
    as a home.
I dispelled his disappointment. Santa Claus will
    not refuse.
For your father has come, my own dear son. I
    will buy for you new shoes!

THE MAN ON THE FLYING TRAPEZE

A short while ago this enduring ballad had a country-wide revival. I remember its being sung in a circus when I was very young. How long ago was that? I have nothing to say.

Once I was happy, but now I'm forlorn,
Like an old coat, all tattered and torn,
Left in this wide world to fret and to mourn,
Betrayed by a maid in her teens.
Oh, the girl that I loved she was handsome,
I tried all I knew her to please,
But I could not please one quarter as well
As the man on the flying trapeze.

CHORUS

He would fly through the air
With the greatest of ease,
This daring young man
On the flying trapeze;
His movements were graceful,
All girls he could please,
And my love he purloined away.

Her father and mother were both on my side,
And very hard tried to make her my bride.
Her father he sighed, and her mother she cried
To see her throw herself away.
'Twas all no avail, she'd go there every night
And throw him bouquets on the stage,
Which caused him to meet her; how he ran me
  down
To tell you would take a whole page.

One night I as usual called at her dear home,
Found there her father and mother alone.
I asked for my love, and soon they made known
To my horror that she'd run away.
She packed up her goods and eloped in the night
With him with the greatest of ease;
From three stories high he had lowered her down
To the ground on his flying trapeze.

Some months after this, I chanced in a hall,
Was greatly surprised to see on the wall
A bill in red letters that did my heart gall,
That she was appearing with him.
He taught her gymnastics and dressed her in
  tights
To help him to live at his ease,
And made her assume a masculine name,
And now she goes on the trapeze.

CHORUS

She floats through the air
With the greatest of ease,
You'd think her a man
On the flying trapeze.
She does all the work
While he takes his ease,
And that's what became of my love.
                                    —*Unknown*

THE GIRL WITH THE BLUE VELVET BAND

by John F. Leonard

When Captain Billy Fawcett published his famous
Smokehouse Poetry, he revived this once great favorite and
made it more popular than ever. He had to reprint it many
times.

In that city of wealth, beauty and fashion;
Dear old Frisco, where I first saw the light,
And the many frolics that I had there
Are still fresh in my memory tonight.

One evening while out for a ramble;
Here or there without thought or design,
I chanced on a young girl, tall and slender,
At the corner of Kearney and Pine.

On her face was the first flush of nature,
And her bright eyes seemed to expand;
While her hair fell in rich, brilliant masses,
Was entwined in a blue velvet band.

To a house of gentle ruination,
She invited me with a sweet smile;
She seemed so refined, gay and charming
That I thought I would tarry a while.

She then shared with me a collection
Of wines of an excellent brand,
And conversed in politest language;
The Girl with the Blue Velvet Band.

After lunch, to a well-kept apartment,
We repaired to the third floor above;
And I thought myself truly in Heaven,
Where reigneth the Goddess of Love.

Her lady's taste was resplendent,
From the graceful arrangement of things;
From the pictures that stood on the bureau,
To a little bronze Cupid with wings.

But what struck me the most was an object
Designed by an artistic hand;
'Twas the costly "lay-out" of a hop-fiend,
And that fiend was my Blue Velvet Band.

On a pile of soft robes and pillows,
She reclined, I declare, on the floor,
Then we both hit the pipe and I slumbered,
I ponder it o'er and o'er.

'Tis months since the craven arm grasped me,
And in bliss did my life glide away;
From opium to "dipping" and thieving,
She artfully led day by day.

One evening, coming home wet and dreary,
With the swag from a jewelry store,
I heard the soft voice of my loved one,
As I gently opened the door.

"If you'll give me a clue to convict him,"
Said a stranger, in tones soft and bland,
"You'll then prove to me that you love me."
"It's a go," said my Blue Velvet Band.

Ah! How my heart filled with anger,
At woman, so fair, false and vile,
And to think that I once true adored her;
Brought to my lips a contemptible smile.

All ill-gotten gains we had squandered,
And my life was hers to command;
Betrayed and deserted for another—
Could this be my Blue Velvet Band?

Just a few moments before I was hunted
By the cops, who wounded me, too,
And my temper was none the sweetest,
As I swung myself into their view.

And the copper, not liking the glitter
Of the "44" Colt in my hand,
Hurriedly left through the window,
Leaving me with my Blue Velvet Band.

What happened to me I will tell you;
I was "ditched" for a desperate crime;
There was hell in a bank about midnight,
And my pal was shot down in his prime.

As a convict of hard reputation,
Ten years of hard grind I did land,
And I often thought of the pleasures
I had with my Blue Velvet Band.

One night as bedtime was ringing,
I was standing close to the bars,
I fancied I heard a girl singing,
Far out in the ocean of stars.

Her voice had the same touch of sadness
I knew that but one could command,
It had the same thrill of gladness
As that of my Blue Velvet Band.

Many months have passed since this happened,
And the story belongs to the past;
I forgave her, but just retribution
Claimed this fair but false one at last.

She slowly sank lower and lower,
Down through life's shifting sands,
Till finally she died in a hop joint,
This girl with the Blue Velvet Band.

If she had been true when I met her,
A bright future for us was in store,
For I was an able mechanic,
And honest and square to the core.

But as sages of old have contended,
What's decreed us mortals must stand;
So a grave in the potter's field ended
My romance with the Blue Velvet Band.

Now, when I get out I will hasten
Back to my home town again,
Where my chances are good for some dollars,
All the way from a thousand to ten.

And if I'm in luck I'll endeavor
To live honest in some other land,
And bid farewell to dear old Frisco,
And the grave of my Blue Velvet Band.

★ ★ ★ ★

TO
MAURICE BARRYMORE

by Wilton Lackaye

Maurice Barrymore and Wilton Lackaye, actors of the
highest caliber, were also bosom friends. One night at The
Lambs, New York's famous theatrical club, Bill dashed off
this comment on Barry's genial habit of procrastination.
Luckily I preserved the copy that Bill gave me.

I play beneath the moon.
I sleep beneath the sun.
I promise everything to do
And die with nothing done.

THE PIDDLING PUP

*(A Tale of a Pedigreed Piddlin' Pup in Ten
Piddles and a Puddle)*

I often wondered, when observing George Jean Nathan,
the dean of American drama critics, walking his dog on
44th Street, if he applied the same critical standard to its
performance as he did to that of ordinary dogs.

PIDDLE NO. 1

A farmer's dog came into town,
  His Christian name was Rex,
A noble pedigree had he,
  Unusual was his text.
And as he trotted down the street
  'Twas beautiful to see
His work on every corner—
  His work on every tree.

PIDDLE NO. 2

He watered every gateway too,
  And never missed a post,
For piddling was his specialty
  And piddling was his boast.
The City Curs looked on amazed
  With deep and jealous rage
To see a simple country dog
  The piddler of the age.

PIDDLE NO. 3

Then all the dogs from everywhere
  Were summoned with a yell,
To sniff the country stranger o'er
  And judge him by the smell.
Some thought that he a king might be,
  Beneath his tail a rose,
So every dog drew near to him
  And sniffed it up his nose.

PIDDLE NO. 4

They smelled him over one by one,
  They smelled him two by two,
And noble Rex, in high disdain,
  Stood still till they were thru.
Then just to show the whole shebang
  He didn't give a damn
He trotted in a grocery store
  And piddled on a ham.

PIDDLE NO. 5

He piddled in a mackerel keg—
  He piddled on the floor,
And when the grocer kicked him out
  He piddled through the door.
Behind him all the city dogs
  Lined up with instinct true
To start a piddling carnival
  And see the stranger through.

PIDDLE NO. 6

They showed him every piddling post
  They had in all the town,
And started in with many a wink
  To pee the stranger down.
They sent for champion piddlers
  Who were always on the go,
Who sometimes did a piddling stunt
  Or gave a piddle show.

PIDDLE NO. 7

They sprung these on him suddenly
  When midway in the town;
Rex only smiled and polished off
  The ablest, white or brown.
For Rex was with them every trick
  With vigor and with vim,
A thousand piddles more or less
  Were all the same to him.

27

PIDDLE NO. 8

So he was wetting merrily
  With hind leg kicking high,
When most were hoisting legs in bluff
  And piddling mighty dry.
On and on, Rex sought new grounds
  By piles and scraps and rusts,
Till every city dog went dry
  And piddled only dust.

PIDDLE NO. 9

But on and on went noble Rex
  As wet as any rill,
And all the champion city pups
  Were pee'd to a standstill.
Then Rex did free-hand piddling
  With fancy flirts and flits
Like "double dip" and "gimlet twist"
  And all those latest hits.

PIDDLE NO. 10

And all the time this country dog
  Did never wink or grin,
But piddled blithely out of town
  As he had piddled in.

THE PUDDLE

The city dogs conventions held
  To ask, "What did defeat us?"
But no one ever put them wise
  That Rex had diabetes.

—Unknown

THE ERIE CANAL

When Governor Clinton started the construction of the Erie Canal he was subjected to the usual derision of the mossbacks. They didn't believe it would ever be completed. "If I can live till Clinton's ditch is done I'll die content," was their cynical comment. Many ballads have been written about the canal, but I choose this one as the best.

I've got a mule, her name is Sal,
Fifteen miles on the Erie Canal—
She's a good ol' worker an' a good ol' pal,
Fifteen miles on the Erie Canal—
We've hauled some barges in our day,
Fill'd with lumber, coal and hay,
And we know ev'ry inch of the way
From Albany to Buffalo.

CHORUS

Low bridge, ev'rybody down!
Low bridge, for we're comin' to a town!
And you'll always know your neighbor,
You'll always know your pal,
If you've ever navigated on the Erie Canal.

We better get along on our way, ol' gal,
Fifteen miles on the Erie Canal—
'Cause you bet your life I'd never part with Sal,
Fifteen miles on the Erie Canal.
Git up there, mule, here comes a lock,
We'll make Rome 'bout six o'clock—
One more trip an' back we'll go—
Right back to Buffalo.

—Unknown

THE LITTLE
BROWN JUG

Perhaps the most famous of all drinking ballads—the uninhibited love of a drunkard for his bottle. It has the charm of great honesty.

My wife and I live all alone,
In a little brown hut we call our own,
She loves gin and I love rum,
Tell you what it is, don't we have fun?

CHORUS

Ha, ha, ha! 'Tis you and me,
Little brown jug, don't I love thee?
Ha, ha, ha! 'Tis you and me,
Little brown jug, don't I love thee?

If I had a cow that gave such beer,
I'd dress her in the finest sheer,
Feed her on the choicest hay,
And milk her twenty times a day.

'Tis gin that makes my friends my foes,
'Tis gin that makes me wear old clothes,
But seeing you are so near my nose,
Tip her up and down she goes.

When I go toiling on my farm,
Take little brown jug under my arm,
Set it under some shady tree,
Little brown jug, don't I love thee?

Then came the landlord tripping in,
Round top hat and a peaked chin,
In his hand he carried a cup,
Says I, "Old fellow, give us a sup."

If all the folks in Adam's race
Were put together in one place,
Then I'd prepare to drop a tear
Before I'd part with you, my dear.

—Unknown

* * * *

ALWAYS THE WOMAN PAYS

This is a story that two may tell,
I am the one, the other's in Hell;
A story of amorous burning fire,
With the glamour of love to attune the lyre.

She traveled the road at breakneck speed,
I opened the gates and saddled the steed;
"Ride free!" I cried, and we dashed along,
Her sweet voice echoed a mocking song.

Nights of the wildest revel and mirth,
Days of sorrow, remorse, and dearth,
A heaven of love and a hell of regret
But there's always a woman to pay the debt.

"Sin," says the preacher, "is washed out free,
The blood of the Lamb was shed for thee!"
Smugly I pass the sacred wine,
The woman in Hades pays toll for mine.

I am a pillar of Church and State,
She but the broken sport of Fate;
This is the story that two may tell,
I am the one; the other's in Hell.

—Unknown

THE DEACON'S MASTERPIECE, or THE WONDERFUL "ONE-HOSS SHAY"

by Oliver Wendell Holmes

Have you heard of the wonderful one-hoss shay,
That was built in such a logical way
It ran a hundred years to a day,
And then, of a sudden, it—ah, but stay,
I'll tell you what happened without delay,
Scaring the parson into fits,
Frightening people out of their wits,—
Have you ever heard of that, I say?

Seventeen hundred and fifty-five.
Georgius Secundus was then alive,—
Snuffy old drone from the German hive.
That was the year when Lisbon-town
Saw the earth open and gulp her down,
And Braddock's army was done so brown,
Left without a scalp to its crown.
It was on the terrible Earthquake-day
That the Deacon finished the one-hoss shay.

Now in building of chaises, I tell you what,
There is always *somewhere* a weakest spot,—
In hub, tire, felloe, in spring or thill,
In panel, or crossbar, or floor, or sill,
In screw, bolt, thoroughbrace,—lurking still,
Find it somewhere you must and will,—
Above or below, or within or without,—
And that's the reason, beyond a doubt,
That a chaise *breaks down*, but doesn't *wear out*.

But the Deacon swore (as Deacons do,
With an "I dew vum," or an "I tell *yeou*,")
He would build one shay to beat the taown
'N' the keounty 'n' all the kentry raoun';
It should be so built that it *couldn't* break daown:
—"Fur," said the Deacon, " 't's mighty plain
Thut the weakes' place mus' stan' the strain;
'N' the way t' fix it, uz I maintain,
Is only jest
T' make that place uz strong uz the rest."

So the Deacon inquired of the village folk
Where he could find the strongest oak,
That couldn't be split nor bent nor broke,—
That was for spokes and floor and sills;
He sent for lancewood to make the thills;
The crossbars were ash, from the straightest trees,
The panels of white-wood, that cuts like cheese,
But lasts like iron for things like these;
The hubs of logs from the "Settler's Ellum,"—
Last of its timber,—they couldn't sell 'em,
Never an axe had seen their chips,
And the wedges flew from between their lips,
Their blunt ends frizzled like celery-tips;
Step and prop-iron, bolt and screw,
Spring, tire, axle, and linchpin, too,
Steel of the finest, bright and blue;
Thoroughbrace bison-skin, thick and wide.
Boot, top, dasher, from tough old hide
Found in the pit when the tanner died.
That was the way he "put her through."—
"There!" said the Deacon, "naow she'll dew!"

Do! I tell you, I rather guess
She was a wonder, and nothing less!
Colts grew horses, beards turned gray,
Deacon and Deaconess dropped away,
Children and grandchildren—where were they?
But there stood the stout old one-hoss shay
As fresh as on Lisbon Earthquake-day!
Eighteen hundred;—it came and found
The Deacon's masterpiece strong and sound.
Eighteen hundred increased by ten;—
"Hahnsum kerridge" they called it then.
Eighteen hundred and twenty came;—
Running as usual; much the same.
Thirty and forty at last arrive,
And then come fifty, and fifty-five.

Little of all we value here
Wakes on the morn of its hundredth year
Without both feeling and looking queer.
In fact, there's nothing that keeps its youth,
So far as I know, but a tree and truth.
(This is a moral that runs at large;
Take it.—You're welcome.—No extra charge.)
First of November,—the Earthquake-day—
There are traces of age in the one-hoss shay,
A general flavor of mild decay,
But nothing local, as one may say,
There couldn't be,—for the Deacon's art
Had made it so like in every part
That there wasn't a chance for one to start.
For the wheels were just as strong as the thills,
And the floor was just as strong as the sills,
And the panels just as strong as the floor,
And the whiffle-tree neither less nor more,
And the back cross-bar as strong as the fore,
And spring and axle and hub *encore*.
And yet, *as a whole*, it is past a doubt
In another hour it will be *worn out!*

First of November, 'Fifty-five!
This morning the parson takes a drive.
Now, small boys, get out of the way!
Here comes the wonderful one-hoss shay,
Drawn by a rat-tailed, ewe-necked bay.
"Huddup!" said the parson.—Off went they.

The parson was working his Sunday's text,—
Had got to *fifthly*, and stopped perplexed
At what the—Moses—was coming next.
All at once the horse stood still,
Close by the meet'n'-house on the hill.
—First a shiver, and then a thrill,
Then something decidedly like a spill,—
And the parson was sitting upon a rock,
At half past nine by the meet'n'-house clock,—
Just the hour of the Earthquake's shock!
—What do you think the parson found,
When he got up and stared around?
The poor old chaise in a heap or mound,
As if it had been to the mill and ground!

You see, of course, if you're not a dunce,
How it went to pieces all at once,—
All at once, and nothing first,—
Just as bubbles do when they burst.

End of the wonderful one-hoss shay.
Logic is logic. That's all I say.

THE PASSING OF THE BACKHOUSE

This nostalgic ballad has long been generally attributed to James Whitcomb Riley, one of our most beloved American poets, although his publisher denies Riley's authorship. Whoever wrote it, it has the lilt and feeling of Riley at his best, and is a fitting memorial to a nearly obsolete institution that has succumbed to modern plumbing.

When memory keeps me company and moves to
    smiles or tears,
A weather-beaten object looms through the mist
    of years.
Behind the house and barn it stood, a half mile
    or more,
And hurrying feet a path had made, straight to
    its swinging door.
Its architecture was a type of simple classic art,
But in the tragedy of life it played a leading
    part.
And oft the passing traveler drove slow, and
    heaved a sigh,
To see the modest hired girl slip out with glances
    shy.

We had our posey garden that the women loved
    so well,
I loved it, too, but better still I loved the
    stronger smell
That filled the evening breezes so full of homely
    cheer,
And told the night-o'ertaken tramp that human
    life was near.
On lazy August afternoons, it made a little bower
Delightful, where my grandsire sat and whiled
    away an hour.
For there the summer morning its very cares
    entwined,
And berry bushes reddened in the steaming soil
    behind.

All day fat spiders spun their webs to catch the
    buzzing flies
That flitted to and from the house, where Ma
    was baking pies.
And once a swarm of hornets bold had built a
    palace there,
And stung my unsuspecting aunt—I must not tell
    you where.
Then father took a flaming pole—that was the
    happy day—
He nearly burned the building up, but the hor-
    nets left to stay.
When summer bloom began to fade and winter
    to carouse
We banked the little building with a heap of
    hemlock boughs.

But when the crust was on the snow and the
    sullen skies were gray,
In sooth the building was no place where one
    could wish to stay.
We did our duties promptly, there one purpose
    swayed the mind.
We tarried not, nor lingered long on what we
    left behind.
The torture of that icy seat would make a Spar-
    tan sob,
For needs must scrape the goose-flesh with a
    lacerating cob—
That from a frost-encrusted nail, was suspended
    by a string—
For father was a frugal man and wasted not a
    thing.

When grandpa had to "go out back" and make
    his morning call,
We'd bundle up the dear old man with a muffler
    and a shawl,
I knew the hole on which he sat—'twas padded
    all around,
And once I dared to sit there—'twas all too wide
    I found.
My loins were all too little, and I jack-knifed
    there to stay,
They had to come and get me out, or I'd have
    passed away.
Then father said ambition was a thing that boys
    should shun,
And I just used the children's hole 'till child-
    hood days were done.

And still I marvel at the craft that cut those
    holes so true,
The baby hole, and the slender hole that fitted
    Sister Sue;
That dear old country landmark, I tramped
    around a bit,
And in the lap of luxury my lot has been to sit.
But ere I die I'll eat the fruit of trees I robbed
    of yore,
Then seek the shanty where my name is carved
    upon the door.
I ween the old familiar smell will soothe my
    jaded soul,
I'm now a man, but none the less, I'll try the
    children's hole.

—*Unknown*

★   ★   ★   ★

WAR

by Chief Joseph

of the Nez Percé Tribe

Even Indian chiefs were not immune to the divine
afflatus, as is evidenced by this ballad of lament by Chief
Joseph of the Nez Percé tribe.

Hear me, my warriors; my heart is sick and sad.
Our chiefs are killed,
The old men are all dead.
It is cold, and we have no blankets;
The little children are freezing to death.
Hear me, my warriors; my heart is sick and sad.
From where the sun now stands I will fight no
    more forever!

39

THE MORNIN'S MORNIN'

by Gerald Brennan

Where could you catch better the New York City that
used to be, the city of sidewalks and song, than in this
ballad? Today the old Irish saloons are fighting to keep a
meager foothold on Third Avenue, where once they nestled
door to door and block after block.

This is the tale that Cassidy told
In his halls a-sheen with purple and gold;
Told as he sprawled in an easy chair,
Chewing cigars at a dollar a pair;
Told with a sigh, and perchance a tear,
As the rough soul showed through the cracked
    veneer;
Told as he gazed on the walls nearby,
Where a Greuze and a Millet were hung on high,
With a rude little print in a frame between—
A picture of Shanahan's ould shebeen.

I'm drinkin' me mornin's mornin'—but it doesn't
    tast th' same,
Tho' the glass is iv finest crystal, an' th' liquor
    slips down like a crame,
An' me Cockney footman brings it on a soort of
    a silver plate—
Sherry an' bitters it is, whiskey is out iv date.
In me bran-new brownstone mansion—Fift' Av'-
    noo over th' way—
The cathaydral round th' corner, an' th' Lord
    Archbishop to tay.
Sure I ought to be shtiff wid grandeur, but me
    tastes are mighty mean,
An' I'd rather a mornin's mornin' at Shanahan's
    ould shebeen.

Oh, well do I mind th' shanty—th' rocks an' th'
    field beyant,
The dirt floor yellow wid sawdust, an' th' walls
    on a three-inch slant;
There's a twelve-story flat on the site now—'twas
    meself that builded the same,
An' they called it the Mont-morincy, tho' I
    wanted th' good ould name.
Me dinner pail under me oxther before th'
    whistle blew,
I'd banish the drames from me eyelids wid a nog-
    gin or maybe two;
An' oh, 'twas th' illigant whiskey—its like I have
    never seen
Since I went for me mornin's mornin' to Shana-
    han's ould shebeen.

I disremember th' makers—I couldn't tell you
    the brand,
But it smiled like the golden sunlight, an' it
    looked an' tasted gr-rand.
When me throat was caked wid mortar an' me
    head was cracked wid a blast,
One drink o' Shanahan's dewdrops an' me
    troubles was past.
That's why, as I squat on th' cushins, wid divil a
    hap'orth to do,
In a mornin' coat wid velvit, an' a champagne
    lunch at two,
Th' memory comes like a banshee, meself an' me
    wealth between,
An' I long for a mornin's mornin' in Shanahan's
    ould shebeen.

A mornin' coat lined wid velvit—an' me ould
coat used to do
Alike for mornin' an' evenin' (an' sometimes I
slep' in it, too!),
An' 'twas divil a sup iv sherry that Shanahan
kept—no fear.
If you can't afford good whiskey he'd take you
on trust fer beer.
Th' dacintist gang I knew there—McCarthy (Sin-
athor since),
An' Murphy that mixed the mortar (sure the
Pope has made him a prince).
You should see 'em, avic, o' Sundays, wid faces
scraped an' clean,
When th' boss stood a mornin's mornin' round
Shanahan's ould shebeen.

Whist! Here comes His Grace's carriage, 'twill be
lunchtime by and by,
An' I dasn't drink another—though me throat
is powerful dry;
For I've got to meet th' Archbishop—I'm laborer
now no more,
But ohone, those were fine times then, lad, an'
to talk o' 'em makes me sore.
An' whisper—there's times, I tell you, when I'd
swap this easy chair,
An' the velvit coat an' the footman, wid his Sas-
senach nose in the air,
An' th' Lord Archbishop himself, too, for a drink
o' the days that ha' been,
For the taste o' a mornin's mornin' in Shanahan's
ould shebeen!

FINNIGAN'S WAKE

Irish-American Vaudeville Tune, c. 1870

When I was a boy there was a man in our town called
"Muggy Day" John Doyle. After a "dhrop o' the craythur"
John's rendition of "Finnigan's Wake" was excellent; a
few more, and it was magnificent.

Tim Finnigan lived in Walker Street,
An Irish gentleman mighty odd;
He'd a beautiful brogue so rich and sweet,
And to rise in the world he carried the hod.
But you see, he'd a sort of tippling way,
For the love of the liquor poor Tim was born;
And to help him on his work each day,
He'd a drop of the craythur every morn.

With my philalloo, hubbaboo, whack hurroo,
boys,
Didn't we sing till our jaws did ache,
And shout and laugh and drink and sing,
Oh, it's lots of fun at Finnigan's wake.

One morning Tim was rather full,
His head felt heavy, which made him shake,
He fell from the ladder and broke his skull,
So they carried him home, himself to wake.
They tied him up in a nice clean sheet,
And laid him out upon the bed,
Wid a gallon of whiskey at his feet,
And a barrel of praties at his head.

With my philalloo, hubbaboo, whack hurroo,
boys,
Didn't we sing till our jaws did ache,
And shout and laugh and drink and sing,
Oh, it's lots of fun at Finnigan's wake.

43

His friends assembled at the wake,
Miss Finnigan call'd out for the lunch,
First they brought in tay and cake,
Then pipes, tobacco, and whiskey punch;
Biddy O'Brien began to cry,
Such a pretty corpse she never did see,
Arrah, Tim Mavourneen, why did you die?
"Ah! hould your gab," said Paddy McGree.

With my philalloo, hubbaboo, whack hurroo,
boys,
Didn't we sing till our jaws did ache,
And shout and laugh and drink and sing,
Oh, it's lots of fun at Finnigan's wake.

Then Peggy O'Connor tuck up the job,
"Biddy," says she, "you're wrong, I'm sure,"
But Biddy gave her a pelt in the gob,
And we left her sprawling on the flure;
Oh, then the war did soon enrage!
'Twas woman to woman, and man to man,
Shillelagh law did soon engage!
And a row and a ruction soon began.

With my philalloo, hubbaboo, whack hurroo,
boys,
Didn't we sing till our jaws did ache,
And shout and laugh and drink and sing,
Oh, it's lots of fun at Finnigan's wake.

Then Mickey Mollaney raised his head,
When a gallon of whiskey flew at him,
It missed, an' falling on the bed,
The liquor scatter'd over Tim;
Be-dad he revives, see how he rises,
And Timothy, rising from the bed,
Saying, "Whirl your liquor round like blazes!
Arrah! Gudaguddug, do you think I'm dead?"

*With my philalloo, hubbaboo, whack hurroo,
   boys,
Didn't we sing till our jaws did ache,
And shout and laugh and drink and sing,
Oh, it's lots of fun at Finnigan's wake.*

—*Unknown*

* * * *

BUT I KNOW WHAT I LIKE

by James Montgomery Flagg

Fifty years ago in John Cecil Clay's studio he read me this quatrain by his friend and fellow artist Jimmy Flagg. It was heart-warming to receive Jimmy's permission to include his lethal answer to the Babbitts who spout their opinions on art.

If you chance to be an artist and a person says
      to you
As though it were a sensible remark,
"I don't know anything of Art but know just
      what I like!"
You may answer: "So do monkeys in the park!"

* * * *

Said the Rev. Jabez McCotton:
   "The waltz of the Devil's begotten!"
Said Jones to Miss Bly:
   "Never mind the old guy—
To the Pure almost everything's rotten!"

45

THE BALLAD OF YUKON JAKE

by Edward E. Paramore, Jr.

Imitation may be the sincerest form of flattery, but in parody is also an implicit tribute to the fame of the original. I think Mr. Paramore has paid Robert Service a high compliment in his masterful parody.

Oh, the North Countree is a hard countree
That mothers a bloody brood;
And its icy arms hold hidden charms
For the greedy, the sinful and lewd.
And strong men rust, from the gold and the lust
That sears the Northland soul,
But the wickedest born, from the Pole to the Horn,
Is the Hermit of Shark-Tooth Shoal.

Now Jacob Kaime was the Hermit's name
In the days of his pious youth,
Ere he cast a smirch on the Baptist Church
By betraying a girl named Ruth.
But now men quake at "Yukon Jake,"

The Hermit of Shark-Tooth Shoal,
For that is the name that Jacob Kaime
Is known by from Nome to the Pole.
He was just a boy and the parson's joy
(Ere he fell for the gold and the muck),
And had learned to pray, with the hogs and the
    hay
On a farm near Keokuk.
But a Service tale of illicit kale,
And whisky and women wild,
Drained the morals clean as a soup tureen
From this poor but honest child.

He longed for the bite of a Yukon night
And the Northern Light's weird flicker,
Or a game of stud in the frozen mud,
And the taste of raw red licker.
He wanted to mush along in the slush,
With a team of husky hounds,
And to fire his gat at a beaver hat
And knock it out of bounds.

So he left his home for the hell-town Nome,
On Alaska's ice-ribbed shores,
And he learned to curse and to drink, and worse,
Till the rum dripped from his pores,
When the boys on a spree were drinking it free
In a Malamute saloon
And Dan Megrew and his dangerous crew
Shot craps with the piebald coon;
When the Kid on his stool banged away like a
    fool
At a jag-time melody,
And the barkeep vowed, to the hard-boiled
    crowd,
That he'd cree-mate Sam McGee—

Then Jacob Kaime, who had taken the name
Of Yukon Jake, the Killer,
Would rake the dive with his forty-five
Till the atmosphere grew chiller.
With a sharp command he'd make 'em stand
And deliver their hard-earned dust,
Then drink the bar dry of rum and rye,
As a Klondike bully must.
Without coming to blows he would tweak the
      nose
Of Dangerous Dan Megrew,
And, becoming bolder, throw over his shoulder
The lady that's known as Lou.

Oh, tough as a steak was Yukon Jake—
Hard-boiled as a picnic egg.
He washed his shirt in the Klondike dirt,
And drank his rum by the keg.
In fear of their lives (or because of their wives)
He was shunned by the best of his pals,
An outcast he, from the comradery
Of all but wild animals.
So he bought him the whole of Shark-Tooth
      Shoal,
A reef in the Bering Sea,
And he lived by himself, on a sea lion's shelf
In lonely iniquity.

But, miles away, in Keokuk, Ia.,
Did a ruined maiden fight
To remove the smirch from the Baptist Church
By bringing the heathen Light;
And the Elders declared that all would be spared
If she carried the holy words
From her Keokuk home to the hell-town Nome
To save those sinful birds.
48

So, two weeks later, she took a freighter,
For the gold-cursed land near the Pole,
But Heaven ain't made for a lass that's be-
    trayed—
She was wrecked on Shark-Tooth Shoal!
All hands were tossed in the sea, and lost—
All but the maiden Ruth,
Who swam to the edge of the sea lion's ledge
Where abode the love of her youth.
He was hunting a seal for his evening meal
(He handled a mean harpoon)
When he saw at his feet, not something to eat,
But a girl in a frozen swoon,
Whom he dragged to his lair by her dripping
    hair,
And he rubbed her knees with gin.
To his great surprise, she opened her eyes
And revealed—his Original Sin!

His eight-months beard grew stiff and weird,
And it felt like a chestnut burr,
And he swore by his gizzard and the Arctic
    blizzard
That he'd do right by her.
But the cold sweat froze on the end of her nose
Till it gleamed like a Tecla pearl,
While her bright hair fell, like a flame from hell,
Down the back of the grateful girl.
But a hopeless rake was Yukon Jake,
The Hermit of Shark-Tooth Shoal!
And the dizzy maid he betrayed
And wrecked her immortal soul. . . .
Then he rowed her ashore, with a broken oar,
And he sold her to Dan Megrew
For a husky dog and some hot eggnog,
As rascals are wont to do.

Now ruthless Ruth is a maid uncouth
With scarlet cheeks and lips,
And she sings rough songs to the drunken
    throngs
That come from the sealing ships.
For a rouge-stained kiss from this infamous miss
They will give a seal's sleek fur,
Or perhaps a sable, if they are able;
It's much the same to her.

Oh, the North Countree is a rough countree,
That mothers a bloody brood;
And its icy arms hold hidden charms
For the greedy, the sinful and lewd.
And strong men rust, from the gold and the lust
That sears the Northland soul,
But the wickedest born from the Pole to the
    Horn
Was the Hermit of Shark-Tooth Shoal!

* * * *

A PERSIAN KITTY

Most of us wanted a kitten when we were young. But
the kitten grew into a cat, and the facts of life took our
cherished pet over the back fence.

A Persian kitty, perfumed and fair,
Strayed out through the kitchen door for air,
When a tomcat, lean, and lithe, and strong,
And dirty, and yellow, came along.

He sniffed at the perfumed Persian cat,
As she strutted about with much eclat,
And, thinking a bit of time to pass,
He whispered, "Kiddo, you sure got class."

"That's fitting and proper," was her reply
As she arched the whiskers over her eye.
"I'm ribboned; I sleep on a pillow of silk,
And daily they bathe me in certified milk.

"Yet we're never contented with what we've got,
I try to be happy, but happy I'm not;
And I should be joyful, I should indeed,
For I certainly am highly pedigreed."

"Cheer up," said the tomcat with a smile,
"And trust your new-found friend a while.
You need to escape from your backyard fence.
My dear, all you need is experience."

New joys of life he then unfurled,
As he told her tales of the outside world;
Suggesting at last with a luring laugh
A trip for the two down the Primrose Path.

The morning after the night before,
The cat came back at half past four;
The innocent look in her eyes had went,
But the smile on her face was the smile of
    content.

—Unknown

★ ★ ★ ★

MARY ANNE LOWDER

Here lies the body of Mary Anne Lowder,
She burst while drinking a Seidlitz powder.
Called from this world to her heavenly rest,
She should have waited till it effervesced.

—Unknown

JOHNNY APPLESEED

by William Henry Venable

A Ballad of the Old Northwest

At the very birth of the nineteenth century, if you were
one of the pioneers scattered through the Ohio territory
you might have been greeted by a young man appearing
out of nowhere. He would be leading a horse, bearing bags
of apple seeds on its back. That was Jonathan Chapman,
known in every log cabin in the territory as Johnny Appleseed. There are apple orchards bearing today that were
planted by Johnny.

A midnight cry appalls the gloom,
    The puncheon door is shaken:
"Awake! arouse! and flee the doom!
    Man, woman, child, awaken!

"Your sky shall glow with fiery beams
    Before the morn breaks ruddy!
The scalpknife in the moonlight gleams,
    Athirst for vengeance bloody!"

Alarumed by the dreadful word
    Some warning tongue thus utters,
The settler's wife, like mother bird,
    About her young ones flutters.

Her first-born, rustling from a soft
    Leaf-couch, the roof close under,
Glides down the ladder from the loft,
    With eyes of dreamy wonder.

The pioneer flings open wide
    The cabin door naught fearing;
The grim woods drowse on every side,
    Around the lonely clearing.

"Come in! come in! not like an owl
    Thus hoot your doleful humors;
What fiend possesses you to howl
    Such crazy, coward rumors!"

The herald strode into the room;
    That moment, through the ashes,
The back-log struggled into bloom
    Of gold and crimson flashes.

The glimmer lighted up a face,
    And o'er a figure dartled,
So eerie, of so solemn grace,
    The bluff backwoodsman startled.

The brow was gathered to a frown,
    The eyes were strangely glowing,
And, like a snow-fall drifting down,
    The stormy beard went flowing.

The tattered cloak that round him clung
    Had warred with foulest weather;
Across his shoulders broad were flung
    Brown saddlebags of leather.

One pouch with hoarded seed was packed,
    From Penn-land cider presses;
The other garnered book and tract
    Within its creased recesses.

A glance disdainful and austere,
    Contemptuous of danger,
Cast he upon the pioneer,
    Then spake the uncouth stranger:

"Heed what the Lord's anointed saith;
    Hear one who would deliver
Your bodies and your souls from death;
    List ye to John the Giver.

"Thou trustful boy, in spirit wise
  Beyond thy father's measure,
Because of thy believing eyes
  I share with thee my treasure.

"Of precious seed this handful take;
  Take next this Bible Holy:
In good soil sow both gifts, for sake
  Of Him, the meek and lowly.

"Farewell! I go!—the forest calls
  My life to ceaseless labors;
Wherever danger's shadow falls
  I fly to save my neighbors.

"I save; I neither curse nor slay;
  I am a voice that crieth
In night and wilderness. Away!
  Whoever doubteth, dieth!"

The prophet vanished in the night,
  Like some fleet ghost belated:
Then, awe-struck, fled with panic fright
  The household, evil-fated.

They hurried on with stumbling feet,
  Foreboding ambuscado;
Bewildered hope told of retreat
  In frontier palisado.

But ere a mile of tangled maze
  Their bleeding hands had broken,
Their home-roof set the dark ablaze,
  Fulfilling doom forespoken.

The savage death-whoop rent the air!
  A howl of rage infernal!
The fugitives were in Thy care,
  Almighty Power eternal!

Unscathed by tomahawk or knife,
  In bosky dingle nested,
The hunted pioneer, with wife
  And babes, hid unmolested.

The lad, when age his locks of gold
  Had changed to silver glory,
Told grandchildren, as I have told,
  This western wildwood story.

Told how the fertile seeds had grown
  To famous trees, and thriven;
And oft the Sacred Book was shown,
  By that weird Pilgrim given.

Remember Johnny Appleseed,
  All ye who love the apple,
He served his kind by Word and Deed,
  In God's grand greenwood chapel.

★　★　★　★

I'VE BEEN WORKIN'
ON THE RAILROAD

I've been workin' on the railroad
All the livelong day.
I've been workin' on the railroad
Just to pass the time away.
Don't you hear the whistle blowing?
Rise up so early in the morn.
Don't you hear the Captain shouting:
"Dinah, blow your horn."

—Unknown

WHERE IS YOUR BOY TONIGHT?

Life is teeming with evil snares,
The gates of sin are wide,
The rosy fingers of pleasure wave,
And beckon the young inside.
Man of the world with open purse,
Seeking your own delight,
Pause ere reason is wholly gone—
Where is your boy tonight?

Sirens are singing on every hand,
Luring the ear of youth,
Gilded falsehood with silver notes
Drowneth the voice of truth.
Dainty ladies in costly robes,
Your parlours gleam with light,
Fate and beauty your senses steep—
Where is your boy tonight?

Tempting whispers of royal spoil
Flatter the youthful soul
Eagerly entering into life,
Restive of all control.
Needs are many, and duties stern
Crowd on the weary sight;
Father, buried in business cares,
Where is your boy tonight?

Pitfalls lurk in the flowery way,
Vice has a golden gate:
Who shall guide the unwary feet
Into the highway straight?
Patient worker with willing hand,
Keep the home hearth bright,
Tired mother, with tender eyes—
Where is your boy tonight?

Turn his feet from the evil paths
Ere they have entered in:
Keep him unspotted while yet he may,
Earth is so stained with sin;
Ere he has learned to follow wrong,
Teach him to love the right;
Watch ere watching is wholly vain—
Where is your boy tonight?

—*Unknown*

* * * *

OPPORTUNITY

by John J. Ingalls

John J. Ingalls was a Kansas lawyer, editor, and an incorruptible United States Senator, as certain railroads discovered when they tried to bribe him. He also covered the Corbett-Fitzsimmons fight for the newspapers. "Opportunity" may cause discussion as to its philosophy, but no one can question its stature.

Master of human destinies am I!
    Fame, love and fortune on my footsteps wait.
    Cities and fields I walk: I penetrate
Deserts and fields remote, and, passing by
    Hovel and mart and palace, soon or late
    I knock unbidden once at every gate!
If sleeping, wake: if feasting, rise before
    I turn away. It is the hour of fate,
    And they who follow me reach every state
Mortals desire, and conquer every foe
    Save death; but those who doubt or hesitate,
Condemned to failure, penury and woe,
    Seek me in vain and uselessly implore—
    I answer not, and I return no more.

57

ABDULLAH BULBUL AMIR

The sons of the Prophet are valiant and bold,
  And quite unaccustomed to fear;
And the bravest of all was a man, so I'm told,
  Called Abdullah Bulbul Amir.

When they wanted a man to encourage the van,
  Or harass the foe from the rear,
Storm fort or redoubt, they were sure to call out
  For Abdullah Bulbul Amir.

There are heroes in plenty, and well known to
    fame,
  In the legions that fight for the Czar;
But none of such fame as the man by the name
  Of Ivan Petrofsky Skovar.

He could imitate Irving, tell fortunes by cards,
  And play on the Spanish guitar;
In fact, quite the cream of the Muscovite guards
  Was Ivan Petrofsky Skovar.

One day this bold Muscovite shouldered his gun,
  Put on his most cynical sneer,
And was walking downtown when he happened
    to run
  Into Abdullah Bulbul Amir.

"Young man," said Bulbul, "is existence so dull
  That you're anxious to end your career?
Then, infidel, know you have trod on the toe
  Of Abdullah Bulbul Amir.

"So take your last look at the sea, sky and brook,
  Make your latest report on the war;
For I mean to imply you are going to die,
  O Ivan Petrofsy Skovar."

So this fierce man he took his trusty chibouk,
  And murmuring, "Allah Akbar!"
With murder intent he most savagely went
  For Ivan Petrofsky Skovar.

The Sultan rose up, the disturbance to quell,
  Likewise, give the victor a cheer.
He arrived just in time to bid hasty farewell
  To Abdullah Bulbul Amir.

A loud-sounding splash from the Danube was
    heard
  Resounding o'er meadows afar;
It came from the sack fitting close to the back
  Of Ivan Petrofsky Skovar.

There lieth a stone where the Danube doth roll,
  And on it in characters queer
Are "Stranger, when passing by, pray for the
    soul
  Of Abdullah Bulbul Amir."

A Muscovite maiden her vigil doth keep
  By the light of the pale northern star,
And the name she repeats every night in her
    sleep
  Is Ivan Petrofsky Skovar.

—Unknown

* * * *

BILLY BOY

Oh, where have you been, Billy boy, Billy boy,
Oh, where have you been, charming Billy?
I have been to seek a wife, she's the joy of my
    young life,
She's a young thing and cannot leave her mother.

Did she ask you to come in, Billy boy, Billy boy,
Did she ask you to come in, charming Billy?
She did ask me to come in, with a dimple in her
    chin,
She's a young thing and cannot leave her mother.

Did she ask you to sit down, Billy boy, Billy boy,
Did she ask you to sit down, charming Billy?
She did ask me to sit down, with a curtsey to
    the ground,
She's a young thing and cannot leave her mother.

Did she set for you a chair, Billy boy, Billy boy,
Did she set for you a chair, charming Billy?
Yes, she set for me a chair, she's got ringlets
    in her hair,
She's a young thing and cannot leave her mother.

How old is she, Billy boy, Billy boy,
How old is she, charming Billy?
She's three times six, four times seven, twenty-
    eight and eleven,
She's a young thing and cannot leave her mother.

How tall is she, Billy boy, Billy boy,
How tall is she, charming Billy?
She's as tall as any pine and as straight's a pump-
kin vine,
She's a young thing and cannot leave her mother.

Can she make a cherry pie, Billy boy, Billy boy,
Can she make a cherry pie, charming Billy?
She can make a cherry pie, quick's a cat can
wink her eye,
She's a young thing and cannot leave her mother.

Does she often go to church, Billy boy, Billy boy,
Does she often go to church, charming Billy?
Yes, she often goes to church, with her bonnet
white as birch,
She's a young thing and cannot leave her mother.

Can she make a pudding well, Billy boy, Billy
boy,
Can she make a pudding well, charming Billy?
She can make a pudding well, I can tell it by
the smell,
She's a young thing and cannot leave her mother.

Can she make a feather-bed, Billy boy, Billy boy,
Can she make a feather-bed, charming Billy?
She can make a feather-bed, place the pillows
at the head,
She's a young thing and cannot leave her mother.

Can she card and can she spin, Billy boy, Billy
boy,
Can she card and can she spin, charming Billy?
She can card and she can spin, she can do most
anything,
She's a young thing and cannot leave her mother.

—*Unknown*

LASCA

by Frank Desprez

"Lasca" will persist through the years as one of America's finest and most dramatic ballads. Love, hatred, and courage are vividly set down here for our enjoyment.

I want free life, and I want fresh air;
And I sigh for the canter after the cattle,
The crack of the whips like shots in battle,
The medley of hoofs and horns and heads
That wars and wrangles and scatters and
    spreads;
The green beneath and the blue above,
And dash and danger, and life and love—
And Lasca!
            Lasca used to ride
On a mouse-grey mustang close by my side,
With blue serape and bright-belled spur;
I laughed with joy as I looked at her!
Little knew she of books or creeds;
An Ave Maria sufficed her needs;
Little she cared save to be at my side,
To ride with me, and ever to ride,
From San Saba's shore to Lavaca's tide.
She was as bold as the billows that beat,
She was as wild as the breezes that blow:
From her little head to her little feet,
She was swayed in her suppleness to and fro
By each gust of passion; a sapling pine
That grows on the edge of a Kansas bluff
And wars with the wind when the weather is
    rough,
Is like this Lasca, this love of mine.

She would hunger that I might eat,
Would take the bitter and leave me the sweet;
But once, when I made her jealous for fun
At something I whispered or looked or done,
One Sunday, in San Antonio,
To a glorious girl in the Alamo,
She drew from her garter a little dagger,
And—sting of a wasp—it made me stagger!
An inch to the left, or an inch to the right,
And I shouldn't be maundering here tonight;
But she sobbed, and sobbing, so quickly bound
Her torn reboso about the wound
That I swiftly forgave her. Scratches don't count
     In Texas, down by the Rio Grande.

Her eye was brown—a deep, deep brown;
Her hair was darker than her eye;
And something in her smile and frown,
Curled crimson lip and instep high,
Showed that there ran in each blue vein,
Mixed with the milder Aztec strain,
The vigorous vintage of Old Spain.
She was alive in every limb
With feeling, to the finger tips;
And when the sun is like a fire,
And sky one shining, soft sapphire
One does not drink in little sips.

The air was heavy, the night was hot,
I sat by her side and forgot, forgot;
Forgot the herd that were taking their rest,
Forgot that the air was close oppressed,
That the Texas norther comes sudden and soon,
In the dead of the night or the blaze of the noon;
That, once let the herd at its breath take fright,
Nothing on earth can stop their flight;
And woe to the rider, and woe to the steed,
That falls in front of their mad stampede!

Was that thunder? I grasped the cord
Of my swift mustang without a word.
I sprang to the saddle, and she clung behind.
Away! on a hot chase down the wind!
But never was fox-hunt half so hard,
And never was steed so little spared.
For we rode for our lives. You shall hear how
    we fared
       In Texas, down by the Rio Grande.

The mustang flew, and we urged him on;
There was one chance left, and you have but
    one—
Halt, jump to the ground, and shoot your horse;
Crouch under his carcass, and take your chance;
And if the steers in their frantic course
Don't batter you both to pieces at once,
You may thank your star; if not, goodbye
To the quickening kiss and the long-drawn sigh,
And the open air and the open sky,
       In Texas, down by the Rio Grande.

The cattle gained on us, and just as I felt
For my old six-shooter behind in my belt,
Down came the mustang, and down came we,
Clinging together—and, what was the rest?
A body that spread itself on my breast,
Two arms that shielded my dizzy head,
Two lips that hard to my lips were prest;
Then came thunder in my ears,
As over us surged the sea of steers,
Blows that beat blood into my eyes,
And when I could rise—
Lasca was dead!

I gouged out a grave a few feet deep,
And there in the Earth's arms I laid her to sleep;
And there she is lying, and no one knows;
And the summer shines, and the winter snows;
For many a day the flowers have spread
A pall of petals over her head;
And the little grey hawk hangs aloft in the air,
And the sly coyote trots here and there,
And the black snake glides and glitters and
    slides
Into the rift of a cottonwood tree;
And the buzzard sails on,
And comes and is gone,
Stately and still, like a ship at sea.
And I wonder why I do not care
For the things that are, like the things that
    were.
Does half my heart lie buried there
    In Texas, down by the Rio Grande?

★   ★   ★   ★

DO YOU KNOW HOW MANY STARS?

Do you know how many stars
There are shining in the skies?
Do you know how many clouds
Ev'ry day go floating by?
God in heaven has counted all,
He would miss one should it fall.

Do you know how many children
Go to little beds at night,
And without a care or sorrow,
Wake up in the morning light?
God in heaven each name can tell,
Loves you, too, and loves you well.

—*Unknown*

MOTHER'S LETTER

You may write a thousand letters
To the girlie you adore
And declare in every letter
That you love her more and more;
You may praise her grace and beauty
In a thousand glowing lines
And compare her eyes of azure
With the brightest star that shines.
If you had the pen of Shakespeare
You would use it every day
In composing written worship
To that sweetheart far away;
But a letter far more welcome
To an older, gentler breast,
Is a letter to a mother
From the boy she loves the best.

Youthful blood is fierce and flaming
And when writing to your love
You will rave about devotion
Swearing by the stars above,
Vowing by the moon's white splendor
That the girlie you adore
Is the one you'll ever cherish
As no maid was loved before,
You will pen full many a promise
On those pages white and dumb,
That you never can live up to
In the married years to come,
But a letter far more precious,
Bringing more and sweeter bliss,
Is the one that's penned to mother
From the lad she yearns to kiss.

She is the best friend that you have,
No matter what you say;
She'll always heed your calling,
Be it either night or day.
Your dad may turn against you,
Your brother, sister, too,
But mother—she'll stand by you
No matter what you do.
Her dear old heart is aching,
Each night she breathes a prayer
That God will bless her darling
And be with him everywhere;
Her heart grows much more tender
As her hair shows streaks of gray;
So sit down, boys, and send her
A line or two today.

Regardless of its diction,
Its spelling or its style,
Although the composition
Might provoke a critic's smile,
She will read it very often
When the lights are soft and low,
Seated in the same old corner
Where she nursed you years ago.
In her old and trembling fingers
It becomes a work of art,
Stained with tears of joy and gladness
As she breathes, "God bless his heart."
Yes, the letter of all letters,
Look wherever you may roam,
Is a letter to a mother
From her son away from home.

—*Unknown*

ANNIE BREEN

Come all ye men of Arkansas, a tale to you I'll
    sing,
Of Annie Breen from old Kaintuck who made
    the forest ring.
For sweeter gal and sweeter voice no man did
    ever know,
And well she loved a straight-limbed lad whose
    name was Texas Joe.

To meetin' she and Joe they went, and oh, her
    eyes did shine,
To see him full of manly strength, so clear and
    tall and fine.
To be his wife and helping hand she wanted
    as her fate,
But sad the story that befell as now I will relate.

One morn when birds were singin' an' the lilacs
    were abloom,
There came unto the little town and there he
    took a room,
An evil-hearted city man who said he'd made
    his stake,
And then it was that the serpent in the Paradise
    did wake.

At meetin' after prayers were said, sweet Ann
    sang clear and fine.
The stranger said upon his knees, "That girl she
    must be mine."
So arm in arm they both walked home and wan-
    dered up and down,
Which caused the neighbors, who loved Ann, to
    shake their heads and frown.

He entered in and brought a stain on Annie
    Breen's fair life.
He told her that he loved the girl, would take
    her for his wife.
When Joe got wind how matters stood his heart
    was like a stone,
With ne'er a word of parting he went off to
    Texas alone.

Before a year in a shallow grave lay Annie and
    her child,
But when the tidings reached brave Joe's ears
    that lad went almost wild.
He saddled up and cantered hard, and rode both
    long and fast
And in Fort Smith he found the man who'd
    ruined Ann at last.

Then words were spoke and shots were fired and
    Joe fell on the floor,
He said, "In spite of all that's been I love my
    Ann the more."
His face was white as driven snow, his breath
    came gasping low,
He said, "My soul is clean and to my Maker
    it must go."

Before he closed his dimming eye he said, "My
    work's not done,"
And turning on his aching side he drew his
    faithful gun.
"You've done your mischief, stranger, but from
    life you've got to part."
His finger pressed the trigger and he shot him
    through the heart.

—*Unknown*

BALLAD

by Abraham Lincoln

Perhaps you share my conviction that a great statesman
must have a song in his heart. Take this untitled ballad
written by Lincoln at the age of thirty-seven. Judging from
his letters, he wrote many more that were destroyed, with
other Lincolniana, by people who should never have been
born.

My childhood's home I see again,
　And sadden with the view;
And still, as memory crowds my brain,
　There's pleasure in it too.

O Memory! thou midway world
　'Twixt earth and paradise,
Where things decayed and loved ones lost
　In dreamy shadows rise,

And, freed from all that's earthly vile,
　Seem hallowed, pure and bright,
Like scenes in some enchanted isle
　All bathed in liquid light.

As dusky mountains please the eye
　When twilight chases day;
As bugle-notes that passing by,
　In distance die away;

As leaving some grand waterfall,
　We, lingering, list its roar—
So memory will hallow all
　We've known but know no more.

Near twenty years have passed away
    Since here I bid farewell
To woods and fields, and scenes of play,
    And playmates loved so well.

Where many were, but few remain
    Of old familiar things;
But seeing them to mind again
    The lost and absent brings.

The friends I left that parting day,
    How changed, as time has sped!
Young childhood grown, strong manhood gray;
    And half of all are dead.

I hear the loved survivors tell
    How nought from death could save,
Till every sound appears a knell,
    And every spot a grave.

I range the fields with pensive tread,
    And pace the hollow rooms,
And feel (companion of the dead)
    I'm living in the tombs.

* * * *

AMERICA GREETS AN ALIEN

Hail, guest! We ask not what thou art.
If friend, we greet thee hand and heart;
If stranger, such no longer be;
If foe, our love shall conquer thee.

—*Unknown*

NATCHEZ NAN AND HER GAMBLING MAN

by C. H. Wheeler

Derringer Dan was a gambling man
  Who plied his trade on the Nellie Bly,
Whose paddles dipped in the Mississipp
  As the swampy banks slid by.
The backs he glimmed as the cards he skimmed
  With never a crooked move;
Early and late he shuffled them straight,
  For his heart held naught but love.

The guiding force who mapped his course
  Was his sweetheart, Natchez Nan;
The captain's daughter who loved the water,
  And worshipped Derringer Dan,
As with smiling lips he stacked his chips
  In towers blue, white, and red.
She lived in dreams of New Orleans
  And the day when they would wed.

The whistle blew for Belle Bayou
  With its landing piled with bales;
The lusty shouts of the roustabouts
  Answered the planter's hails.
Then up the plank with swagger and swank
  Came a gent with a long moustache,
Clerical frock, and a pearl in his stock,
  Who looked like ready cash.

Handsome Hank strolled up the plank—
    A pearler, rake, and scamp;
A "nigger robber" and "poker dauber,"
    From an up-state mussel camp.
He bartered pearls with crib-line girls
    At "Natchez Under the Hill,"
And would oft' flim-flam a digger of clams;
    In fact, he'd been known to kill.

Natchez Nan watched Derringer Dan
    When Hank horned into the game.
She heard Dan say in his quiet way,
    "My friend, I have heard your fame
As a wizard at cards in the mussel yards,
    So forgive me if I must chide.
Retain your gloves, but your coat remove—
    Those sleeves are much too wide!"

Nan saw the flash, the crimson splash,
    As Dan sank to the floor;
With a panther's glide she stood beside
    Her love who lived no more.
He faced his God, but his two-barreled rod
    Was safe in the hand of Nan,
Who slammed a ball in the cabin wall
    Through the heart of the pearler man.

"Your game was rank," she sneered at Hank,
    " 'Twas a rotten card you played.
You yellow scum, you lousy bum,
    Your last draw is a spade.
You did away with my fiancé,
    Now we'll follow him on his trip."
And the captain's daughter who loved the water
    Hopped into the Mississipp.

THE DEAD MEN'S SONG

by Young Ewing Allison

I suppose there are many different versions of this ballad in every English-speaking country and perhaps even in other countries too. This is my favorite.

Fifteen men on the Dead Man's Chest,
  Yo-ho-ho and a bottle of rum!
Drink and the devil had done for the rest,
  Yo-ho-ho and a bottle of rum!
The mate was fixed by the bo'sun's pike
An' the bo'sun brained with a marlin-spike,
And the cookie's throat was marked belike
It had been clutched by fingers ten.
And there they lay, all good dead men,
Like break o' day in a boozin' ken—
  Yo-ho-ho and a bottle of rum!

Fifteen men of the whole ship's list,
  Yo-ho-ho and a bottle of rum!
Dead and bedamned and their souls gone whist,
  Yo-ho-ho and a bottle of rum!
The skipper lay with his nob in gore
Where the scullion's axe his cheek had shore,
And the scullion he was stabbed times four;
And there they lay, and the soggy skies
Dripped ceaselessly in upstaring eyes,
By murk sunset and by foul sunrise—
  Yo-ho-ho and a bottle of rum!

Fifteen men of 'em stiff and stark,
   Yo-ho-ho and a bottle of rum!
Ten of the crew bore the murder mark,
   Yo-ho-ho and a bottle of rum!
'Twas a cutlass swipe or an ounce of lead,
Or a gaping hole in a battered head,
And the scuppers' glut of a rotting red.
And there they lay, ay, damn my eyes,
Their lookouts clapped on Paradise,
Their souls gone just the contrawise—
   Yo-ho-ho and a bottle of rum!

Fifteen men of 'em good and true,
   Yo-ho-ho and a bottle of rum!
Every man Jack could 'a' sailed with Old Pew,
   Yo-ho-ho and a bottle of rum!
There was chest on chest of Spanish gold
And a ton of plate in the middle hold,
And the cabin's riot of loot untold—
And there they lay that had took the plum,
With sightless eyes and with lips struck dumb,
And we shared all by rule o' thumb—
   Yo-ho-ho and a bottle of rum!

More was seen through the stern light's screen,
   Yo-ho-ho and a bottle of rum!
Chartings ondoubt where a woman had been,
   Yo-ho-ho and a bottle of rum!
A flimsy shift on a bunker cot
With a dirk slit sheer through the bosom spot
And the lace stiff dry in a purplish rot—
Or was she wench or shuddering maid,
She dared the knife and she took the blade—
Faith, there was stuff for a plucky jade!
   Yo-ho-ho and a bottle of rum!

Fifteen men on the Dead Man's Chest,
  Yo-ho-ho and a bottle of rum!
Drink and the devil had done for the rest,
  Yo-ho-ho and a bottle of rum!
We wrapped 'em all in a mainsail tight,
With twice ten turns of a hawser's bight,
And we heaved 'em over and out of sight,
With a yo-heave-ho and a fare-ye-well,
And a sullen plunge in a sullen swell,
Ten fathoms along on the road to hell—
  Yo-ho-ho and a bottle of rum!

★　★　★　★

HAD A SET OF
DOUBLE TEETH

by Holman F. Day

Oh, listen while I tell you a truthful little tale
  Of a man whose teeth were double all the
    solid way around;
He could jest as slick as preachin' bite in two a
    shingle-nail,
  Or squonch a molded bullet, sah, and ev'ry
    tooth was sound.

I've seen him lift a kag of pork, a-bitin' on the
    chine,
  And he'd clench a rope and hang there like a
    puppy to a root;
And a feller he could pull and twitch and yank
    up on the line,
  But he couldn't do no business with that dou-
    ble-toothed galoot.

77

He was luggin' up some shingles,—bunch, sah,
    underneath each arm,—
  The time that he was shinglin' of the Baptist
    meetin'-house;
The ladder cracked and buckled, but he didn't
    think no harm,
  When all at once she busted, and he started
    down kersouse.

His head, sah, when she busted, it was jest
    abreast the eaves;
  And he nipped, sah, quicker'n lightnin', and
    he gripped there with his teeth,
And he never dropped the shingles, but he hung
    to both the sheaves,
  Though the solid ground was suttenly more'n
    thirty feet beneath.

He held there and he kicked there and he
    squirmed, but no one come;
  He was workin' on the roof alone—there warn't
    no folks around—
He hung like death to niggers till his jaw was
    set and numb,
  And he reely thought he'd have to drop them
    shingles on the ground.

But all at once old Skillins come a-toddlin' down
    the street;
  Old Skil is sort of hump-backed, and he allus
    looks straight down;
So he never seed the motions of them number
    'leven feet,
  And he went a-amblin' by him—the goramded
    blind old clown!

Now this ere part is truthful—ain't a-stretchin'
   it a mite,—
   When the feller seed that Skillins was a-walkin'
   past the place,
Let go his teeth and hollered, but he grabbed
   back quick and tight,
   'Fore he had a chance to tumble, and hung
   there by the face.

And he never dropped the shingles, and he never
   missed his grip,
   And he stepped out on the ladder when they
   raised it underneath;
And up he went a-flukin' with them shingles on
   his hip,
   And there's the satisfaction of havin' double
   teeth.

*　*　*　*

THE CHARMING YOUNG
WIDOW I MET ON THE
TRAIN

I live in Vermont, and one morning last summer,
   A letter inform'd me my uncle was dead;
   And also requested I'd come down to Boston
   As he'd left me a large sum of money, it said.
Of course I determin'd on making the journey,
   And to book myself by the "first class" I was
   fain
Tho' had I gone "second" I had never en-
   countr'd
   The Charming Young Widow I met on the
   train.

79

Yet scarce was I seated within the compartment,
  Before a fresh passenger entered the door;
'Twas a female, a young one, and dressed in deep
      mourning:
  An infant in long clothes she gracefully bore;
A white cap surrounded a face, oh, so lovely!
  I never shall look on one like it again.
I fell deep in love over head in a moment,
  With the Charming Young Widow I met on
    the train.

The widow and I, side by side, sat together,
  The carriage containing ourselves and no
      more;
When silence was broken by my fair companion,
  Who enquired the time by the watch that I
      wore;
I, of course, satisfied her, and then conversation
  Was freely indulged in by both, till my brain
Fairly reeled with excitement, I grew so en-
    chanted
  With the Charming Young Widow I met on
    the train.

We became so familiar, I ventured to ask her
  How old was the child that she held at her
      breast;
"Ah, sir!" she responded, and into tears bursting,
  Her infant still closer convulsively pressed;
"When I think of my child, I am well nigh dis-
    tracted;
  Its father—my husband—oh, my heart breaks
    with pain."
She, choking with sobs, leaned her head on my
    waistcoat,
  Did the Charming Young Widow I met on
    the train.

By this time the train arrived at a station
    Within a few miles of the great one in town,
When my charmer exclaimed, as she looked
    through the window:
"Good gracious alive! why, there goes Mr.
    Brown.
He's my late husband's brother—dear sir, would
    you kindly
    My best beloved child for a moment sustain?"
Of course, I complied; then off on the platform
    Tripped the Charming Young Widow I met
    on the train.

Three minutes elapsed, then the whistle it
    sounded:
    The train began moving—no widow appeared:
I bawled out, "Stop! stop!" but they paid no
    attention:
    With a snort and a jerk, starting off as I feared;
In the horrid dilemma, I sought for the hour—
    But my watch, ha! where was it? where was
    my chain?
My purse, too, my ticket, gold pencil case, all
    gone,
    Oh, that Artful Young Widow I met on the
    train!

While I was my loss so deeply bewailing,
    The train again stopped, and I "Tickets,
    please," heard;
So I told the conductor, while dandling the in-
    fant,
    The loss I'd sustained, but he doubted my
    word;
He called more officials—a lot gathered round
    me—
    Uncovered the child—oh, how shall I explain?

For behold, 'twas no baby—'twas only a dummy!
 Oh, that Crafty Young Widow I met on the
  train!

Satisfied I'd been robbed, they allowed my de-
  parture,
 Though, of course, I'd settle my fare the next
  day;
And now I wish to counsel young men from the
  country
 Lest they should get served in a similar way.
Beware of young widows you meet on the rail-
  way,
 Who lean on your shoulder—whose tears fall
  like rain;
Look out for your pockets—in case they resemble
 The Charming Young Widow I met on the
  train.

                              —*Unknown*

           ★   ★   ★   ★

WILLIE THE WEEPER

Listen to the story of Willie the Weeper.
Willie the Weeper was a chimney sweeper.
He had the hop habit and he had it bad;
Listen and I'll tell you of a dream he had.

He went to a hop joint the other night,
Where he knew the lights were always shining
  bright,
And, calling for a chink to bring some hop,
He started in smoking like he wasn't gonna stop.

After he'd smoked about a dozen pills,
He said, "This ought to cure all my aches and
  ills."
And turning on his side he fell asleep,
And dreamt he was a sailor on the ocean deep.

He played draw poker as they left the land,
And won a million dollars on the very first hand.
He played and he played till the crew went broke.
Then he turned around and took another smoke.

He came to the island of Siam,
Rubbed his eyes and said, "I wonder where I
  am,"
Played craps with the king and won a million
  more,
But had to leave the island cause the king got
  sore.
He went to Monte Carlo where he played rou-
  lette,
And couldn't lose a penny but won every bet—
Played and he played till the bank went broke.
Then he turned around and took another smoke.

Then he thought he'd better be sailing for home,
And chartered a ship and sailed away alone.
Ship hit a rock. He hit the floor.
Money was gone and the dream was o'er.

Now this is the story of Willie the Weeper;
Willie the Weeper was a chimney sweeper.
Someday a pill too many he'll take,
And dreaming he's dead, he'll forget to awake.

—*Unknown*

THERE IS
A TAVERN

Change the word "tavern" to "night club" and the sentiment is the same as when this classic was written. One thing I'll say for liquor: it has inspired lots of good songs.

There is a tavern in the town,
And there my dear love sits him down, sits him
    down,
And drinks his wine mid laughter free,
And never, never thinks of me.

  Fare thee well for I must leave thee,
  Do not let this parting grieve thee,
  And remember that the best of friends must
    part, must part.

  Adieu, adieu, kind friends, adieu,
  I can no longer stay with you, stay with you,
  I'll hang my harp on the weeping willow tree
  And may the world go well with thee.

He left me for a damsel dark, damsel dark,
Each Friday night they used to spark, used to
  spark,
And now my love once true to me
Takes that dark damsel on his knee.

O dig my grave both wide and deep, wide and
  deep,
Put tombstones at my head and feet, head and
  feet,
And on my breast carve a turtle dove
To signify I died of love.

—Unknown

★　★　★　★

PUNCH, BROTHER, PUNCH

by Isaac H. Bromley

Many besides myself have been under the impression
that Mark Twain wrote this tongue twister. We were
misled by Twain's references to it in "The Atlantic
Monthly" and in "Tom Sawyer Abroad." Investigation
reveals it to be the work of Isaac H. Bromley, inspired by
a sign in the New York horsecars, and published in the
New York Tribune about 1874.

The conductor when he receives a fare
Will punch in the presence of the passinjare,
A blue trip-slip for an 8-cent fare,
A buff trip-slip for a 6-cent fare,
A pink trip-slip for a 3-cent fare,
All in the presence of the passinjare.
Punch, brother, punch, punch with care,
Punch in the presence of the passinjare.

THE EAGLE'S SONG

by Richard Mansfield

Like many other great actors, Richard Mansfield had
other talents. He wrote the novel "Blown Away" and many
excellent verses. "The Eagle's Song" will appeal to intelli-
gent patriots, for whom this book is intended.

The lioness whelped, and the sturdy cub
Was seized by an eagle and carried up,
And homed for a while in an eagle's nest,
And slept for a while on an eagle's breast;
And the eagle taught it the eagle's song:
"To be stanch, and valiant, and free, and strong!"

The lion whelp sprang from the eyrie nest,
From the lofty crag where the queen birds rest;
He fought the King on the spreading plain,
And drove him back o'er the foaming main.
He held the land as a thrifty chief,
And reared his cattle, and reaped his sheaf,
Nor sought the help of a foreign hand,
Yet welcomed all to his own free land!

Two were the sons that the country bore
To the Northern lakes and the Southern shore;
And Chivalry dwelt with the Southern son,
And Industry lived with the Northern one.
Tears for the time when they broke and fought!
Tears was the price of the union wrought!
And the land was red in a sea of blood,
Where brother for brother had swelled the flood!

And now that the two are one again,
Behold on their shield the word "Refrain!"
And the lion cubs twain sing the eagle's song:
"To be stanch, and valiant, and free, and strong!"
For the eagle's beak, and the lion's paw,
And the lion's fangs, and the eagle's claw,
And the eagle's swoop, and the lion's might,
And the lion's leap, and the eagle's sight,
Shall guard the flag with the word "Refrain!"
Now that the two are one again!

* * * *

THE ORPHAN GIRL, or NO BREAD FOR THE POOR

"No home, no home," cried an orphan girl
   At the door of a princely hall,
As she trembling stood on the polished steps
   And leaned on the marble wall.

Her clothes were torn and her head was bare
   And she tried to cover her feet
With her dress that was tattered and covered
      with snow,
   Yes, covered with snow and sleet.

Her dress was thin and her feet were bare
   And the snow had covered her head.
"Oh, give me a home," she feebly cried,
   "A home and a piece of bread."

"My father, alas, I never knew."
   Tears dimmed the eyes so bright.
"My mother sleeps in a new-made grave,
   'Tis an orphan that begs tonight.

"I must freeze," she cried as she sank on the steps
    And strove to cover her feet
With her ragged garments covered with snow,
    Yes, covered with snow and sleet.

The rich man lay on his velvet couch
    And dreamed of his silver and gold
While the orphan girl in her bed of snow
    Was murmuring, "So cold, so cold."

The night was dark and the snow fell fast
    As the rich man closed his door.
And his proud lips curled with scorn as he said,
    "No bread, no room for the poor."

The morning dawned but the orphan girl
    Still lay at the rich man's door
And her soul had fled to that home above
    Where there's bread and room for the poor.

—*Unknown*

* * * *

THE KILKENNY CATS

There wanst was two cats of Kilkenny,
Each thought there was one cat too many,
So they quarreled and they fit,
They scratch'd and they bit,
Till, barrin' their nails,
And the tips of their tails,
Instead of two cats, there warnt any.

—*Unknown*

A STEIN SONG

by Richard Hovey

Give me a rouse, then, in the Maytime
  For a life that knows no fear!
Turn night-time into daytime
  With the sunlight of good cheer!
    For it's always fair weather
    When good fellows get together,
With a stein on the table and a good song ringing
  clear.

When the wind comes up from Cuba,
  And the birds are on the wing,
And our hearts are patting juba
  To the banjo of the spring,
    Then it's no wonder whether
    The boys will get together,
With a stein on the table and a cheer for every-
  thing.

For we're all frank-and-twenty
  When the spring is in the air;
And we've faith and hope a-plenty,
  And we've life and love to spare;
    And it's birds of a feather
    When we all get together,
With a stein on the table and a heart without
  a care.

For we know the world is glorious,
  And the goal a golden thing,
And that God is not censorious
  When His children have their fling;
    And life slips its tether
    When the boys get together,
With a stein on the table in the fellowship of
  spring.

A SONG OF PANAMA

by Alfred Damon Runyon

Forty years ago I listened to Damon Runyon as we sat
in the press box at a game between the Highlanders (now
the Yankees) and the White Elephants (now the Athletics).
He told of his first writings for an Army paper in the
Philippines, while he was a cavalryman chasing the rebel
Aguinaldo. When he became a famous sports writer he
dropped the Alfred from his name. "A Song of Panama"
was inspired by President Theodore Roosevelt's order to
the Canal engineers: "Make the dirt fly!"

"Chuff! chuff! chuff!" An' a mountain bluff
  Is moved by the shovel's song;
"Chuff! chuff! chuff!" Oh, the grade is rough
  A liftin' the landscape along!

We are ants upon a mountain, but we're leavin'
  of our dent,
An' our teeth-marks bitin' scenery they will
  show the way we went;
We're a liftin' half creation, an' we're changin'
  it around,
Just to suit our playful purpose when we're dig-
  gin' in the ground.

"Chuff! chuff! chuff!" Oh, the grade is rough,
  An' the way to the sea is long;
"Chuff! chuff! chuff!" an' the engines puff
  In tune to the shovel's song!

We're a shiftin' miles like inches, and we grab
    a forest here
Just to switch it over yonder so's to leave an
    angle clear;
We're a pushin' leagues o' swamps aside so's we
    can hurry by—
An' if we had to do it we would probably switch
    the sky!

"Chuff! chuff! chuff!" Oh, it's hard enough
    When you're changin' a job gone wrong;
"Chuff! chuff! chuff!" an' there's no rebuff
    To the shovel a singin' its song!

You hears it in the mornin' an' you hears it
    late at night—
It's our battery keepin' action with support o'
    dynamite;
Oh, you gets it for your dinner, an' the scenery
    skips along
In the movin' panorama to the chargin' shovel's
    song!

"Chuff! chuff! chuff!" an' it grabs the scruff
    Of a hill an' boosts it along;
"Chuff! chuff! chuff!" Oh, the grade is rough,
    But it gives to the shovel's song!

This is a fight that's fightin', an' the battle's to
    the death;
There ain't no stoppin' here to rest or even catch
    your breath;
You ain't no noble hero, an' you leave no gallant
    name—
You're a fightin' Nature's army, an' it ain't no
    easy game!

"Chuff! chuff! chuff!" Oh, the grade is rough,
  An' the way to the end is long,
"Chuff! chuff! chuff!" an' the engines puff
  As we lift the landscape along!

★ ★ ★ ★

AFTER THE BALL

by Charles K. Harris

One night at a party at The Lambs club in New York,
I heard Charlie Harris sing his famous ballad in public for
the last time. Some of the younger members had never
heard it before, but they have never forgotten it.

A little maiden climbed an old man's knee,
Begged for a story, "Do, Uncle, please;
Why are you single, why live alone?
Have you no babies, have you no home?"
"I had a sweetheart, years, years ago,
Where she is now, pet, you will soon know.
List to the story, I'll tell it all,
I believed her faithless, after the ball.

CHORUS

"After the ball is over, after the break of morn,
After the dancers' leaving, after the stars are
  gone;
Many a heart is aching, if you could read
  them all;
Many's the hopes that have vanished, after
  the ball.

"Bright lights were flashing in the grand ball-
      room,
Softly the music, playing sweet tunes,
There came my sweetheart, my love, my own,
'I wish some water; leave me alone!'
When I returned, dear, there stood a man,
Kissing my sweetheart as lover can.
Down fell the glass, pet, broken, that's all,
Just as my heart was, after the ball.   (CHORUS)

"Long years have passed, child, I've never wed,
True to my lost love, though she is dead,
She tried to tell me, tried to explain,
I would not listen, pleadings were vain;
One day a letter came, from that man,
He was her brother, the letter ran.
That's why I'm lonely, no home at all,
I broke her heart, pet, after the ball." (CHORUS)

* * * *

THE HELL-BOUND TRAIN

A Texas cowboy on a barroom floor
Had drunk so much he could hold no more;
So he fell asleep with a troubled brain
To dream that he rode on the hell-bound train.

The engine with human blood was damp,
And the headlight was a brimstone lamp;
An imp for fuel was shoveling bones,
And the furnace roared with a thousand groans.

The tank was filled with lager beer,
The devil himself was engineer;
The passengers were a mixed-up crew—
Churchman, atheist, Baptist, Jew;

The rich in broadcloth, poor in rags,
Handsome girls and wrinkled hags;
Black men, yellow, red and white,
Chained together—fearful sight.

The train rushed on at an awful pace
And sulphur fumes burned hands and face;
Wilder and wilder the country grew,
Fast and faster the engine flew.

Loud and terrible thunder crashed.
Whiter, brighter lightning flashed;
Hotter still the air became
Till clothes were burned from each shrinking
    frame.

Then came a fearful ear-splitting yell,
Yelled Satan, "Gents, the next stop's hell!"
'Twas then the passengers shrieked with pain
And begged the devil to stop the train.

He shrieked and roared and grinned with glee,
And mocked and laughed at their misery,
"My friends, you've bought your seats on this
    road
I've got to go through with the complete load.

"You've bullied the weak, you've cheated the
    poor,
The starving tramp you've turned from the door,
You've laid up gold till your purses bust,
You've given play to your beastly lust.

94

"You've mocked at God in your hell-born pride.
You've killed and you've cheated; you've plun-
　　dered and lied,
You've double-crossed men and you've swore and
　　you've stole,
Not a one but has perjured his body and soul.

"So you've paid full fare and I'll carry you
　　through;
If there's one don't belong, I'd like to know who,
And here's the time when I ain't no liar,
I'll land you all safe in the land of fire.

"There your flesh will scorch in the flames that
　　roar,
You'll sizzle and scorch from rind to core."
Then the cowboy awoke with a thrilling cry,
His clothes were wet and his hair stood high.

And he prayed as he never until that hour
To be saved from hell and the devil's power.
His prayers and his vows were not in vain
And he paid no fare on the hell-bound train.

　　　　　　　　　　　　　　—*Unknown*

★　★　★　★

ON CHEESE

by Benjamin Franklin

Jack, eating rotten cheese, did say,
Like Samson I my thousands slay:
I vow, quoth Roger, so you do.
And with the self-same weapon too.

Forgive our women's scornful glance,
Our poor, pale, pure maids decorous,
Virgins by purse and circumstance;
Forgive the tearing tusk and claw;
Forgive the law that made thee thus;
Forgive the God who made the law!

★　★　★　★

THE DOWNFALL OF PIRACY

by Benjamin Franklin

Benjamin Franklin, who caught lightning in a bottle, who wrote "Poor Richard's Almanac," and who was one of America's greatest statesmen, also loved and wrote ballads. We remembered this one from our youth.

Will you hear of a bloody Battle,
　Lately fought upon the Seas?
It will make your Ears to rattle,
　And your Admiration cease;
Have you heard of *Teach* the Rover,
　And his Knavery on the Main;
How of Gold he was a Lover,
　How he lov'd all ill-got Gain?

When the Act of Grace appeared,
　Captain *Teach*, with all his Men,
Unto *Carolina* steered,
　Where they kindly us'd him then;
There he marry'd to a Lady,
　And gave her five hundred Pound,
But to her he prov'd unsteady,
　For he soon march'd off the Ground.

And returned, as I tell you,
  To his Robbery as before,
Burning, sinking Ships of value,
  Filling them with Purple Gore;
When he was at *Carolina*,
  There the Governor did send
To the Governor of *Virginia*,
  That he might assistance lend.

Then the Man-of-War's Commander,
  Two small Sloops he fitted out,
Fifty Men he put on board, Sir,
  Who resolv'd to stand it out;
The Lieutenant he commanded
  Both the Sloops, and you shall hear
How, before he landed,
  He suppress'd them without fear.

Valiant *Maynard* as he sailed,
  Soon the Pirate did espy,
With his Trumpet he then hailed,
  And to him did reply:
Captain *Teach* is our Commander,
  Maynard said, he is the Man
Whom I am resolv'd to hang, Sir,
  Let him do the best he can.

Teach replyed unto *Maynard*,
  You no Quarter here shall see,
But be hang'd on the Mainyard,
  You and all your Company;
Maynard said, I none desire
  Of such Knaves as thee and thine,
None I'll give, *Teach* then replyed,
  My Boys, give me a Glass of Wine.

He took the Glass, and drank Damnation
    Unto *Maynard* and his Crew;
To himself and Generation,
    Then the Glass away he threw;
Brave *Maynard* was resolv'd to have him,
    Tho' he'd Cannons nine or ten;
Teach a broadside quickly gave him,
    Killing sixteen valiant Men.

Maynard boarded him, and to it
    They fell with Sword and Pistol too;
They had Courage, and did show it,
    Killing of the Pirate's Crew.
Teach and *Maynard* on the Quarter,
    Fought it out most manfully,
Maynard's Sword did cut him shorter,
    Losing his head, he there did die.

Every Sailor fought while he, Sir,
    Power had to wield the Sword,
Not a Coward could you see, Sir,
    Fear was driven from aboard;
Wounded Men on both Sides fell, Sir,
    'T was a doleful Sight to see,
Nothing could their Courage quell, Sir,
    O, they fought courageously.

When the bloody Fight was over,
    We're informed by a Letter writ,
Teach's Head was made a Cover,
    To the Jack Staff of the Ship;
Thus they sailed to *Virginia*,
    And when they the Story told,
How they kill'd the Pirates many,
    They'd Applause from young and old.

101

THE FACE ON THE BARROOM FLOOR

by H. Antoine D'Arcy

Hughie D'Arcy always insisted to me that the title of his celebrated work was *not* "The Face on the Barroom Floor" but "The Face on the Floor." I reluctantly bow to popular usage and include "Barroom" in the title. Maurice Barrymore, brilliant father of Ethel, John, and Lionel, spread the ballad's fame by his recitation. Years after, when I was playing with the two boys in "The Jest," Hughie sent them an autographed copy. Seated in his dressing room, Jack read it to Lionel and me with the pathos that only Jack could command.

'Twas a balmy summer evening, and a goodly
    crowd was there,
Which well-nigh filled Joe's barroom on the
    corner of the square,
And as songs and witty stories came through the
    door
A vagabond crept slowly in and posed upon the
    floor.

"Where did it come from?" someone said: "The
    wind has blown it in."
"What does it want?" another cried. "Some
    whisky, rum or gin?"
"Here, Toby, seek him, if your stomach's equal
    to the work—
I wouldn't touch him with a fork, he's filthy as a
    Turk."

This badinage the poor wretch took with stoical
    good grace;
In fact, he smiled as though he thought he'd
    struck the proper place.
"Come, boys, I know there's kindly hearts among
    so good a crowd—
To be in such good company would make a
    deacon proud.

"Give me a drink—that's what I want—I'm out
    of funds, you know;
When I had cash to treat the gang, this hand was
    never slow.
What? You laugh as though you thought this
    pocket never held a sou;
I once was fixed as well, my boys, as any one of
    you.

"There, thanks; that's braced me nicely; God
    bless you one and all;
Next time I pass this good saloon, I'll make an-
    other call.
Give you a song? No, I can't do that, my singing
    days are past;
My voice is cracked, my throat's worn out, and
    my lungs are going fast.

103

"Say! Give me another whisky, and I'll tell you
 what I'll do—
I'll tell you a funny story, and a fact, I promise,
 too.
That I was ever a decent man not one of you
 would think;
But I was, some four or five years back. Say, give
 me another drink.

"Fill her up, Joe, I want to put some life into
 my frame—
Such little drinks, to a bum like me, are misera-
 bly tame;
Five fingers—there, that's the scheme—and cork-
 ing whisky, too.
Well, here's luck, boys; and, landlord, my best
 regards to you.

"You've treated me pretty kindly, and I'd like to
 tell you how
I came to be the dirty sot you see before you
 now.
As I told you, once I was a man, with muscle,
 frame and health,
And, but for a blunder, ought to have made
 considerable wealth.

"I was a painter—not one that daubed on bricks
 and wood
But an artist, and, for my age, was rated pretty
 good.
I worked hard at my canvas and was bidding
 fair to rise,
For gradually I saw the star of fame before my
 eyes.

"I made a picture, perhaps you've seen, 'tis called
the 'Chase of Fame,'
It brought me fifteen hundred pounds and added
to my name.
And then I met a woman—now comes the funny
part—
With eyes that petrified my brain, and sunk into
my heart.

"Why don't you laugh? 'Tis funny that the
vagabond you see
Could ever love a woman and expect her love
for me;
But 'twas so, and for a month or two her smiles
were freely given,
And when her loving lips touched mine it carried
me to heaven.

"Did you ever see a woman for whom your soul
you'd give,
With a form like the Milo Venus, too beautiful
to live;
With eyes that would beat the Koh-i-noor, and
a wealth of chestnut hair?
If so, 'twas she, for there never was another half
so fair.

"I was working on a portrait, one afternoon in
May,
Of a fair-haired boy, a friend of mine, who lived
across the way,
And Madeline admired it, and, much to my
surprise,
Said that she'd like to know the man that had
such dreamy eyes.

"It didn't take long to know him, and before the
    month had flown
My friend had stolen my darling, and I was left
    alone;
And, ere a year of misery had passed above my
    head,
The jewel I had treasured so had tarnished, and
    was dead.

"That's why I took to drink, boys. Why, I never
    saw you smile,
I thought you'd be amused, and laughing all the
    while.
Why, what's the matter, friend? There's a tear-
    drop in your eye,
Come, laugh, like me; 'tis only babes and women
    that should cry.

"Say, boys, if you give me just another whisky,
    I'll be glad,
And I'll draw right here a picture of the face
    that drove me mad.
Give me that piece of chalk with which you
    mark the baseball score—
You shall see the lovely Madeline upon the bar-
    room floor."

Another drink, and with chalk in hand the vaga-
    bond began
To sketch a face that well might buy the soul of
    any man.
Then, as he placed another lock upon the
    shapely head,
With a fearful shriek, he leaped and fell across
    the picture—dead.

BURY ME NOT ON THE LONE PRAIRIE

"O bury me not on the lone prairie!"
These words came low and mournfully
From the pallid lips of a youth who lay
On his dying bed at the close of day.

"O bury me not on the lone prairie,
Where the wild coyotes will howl o'er me,
Where the buzzards beat and the wind goes free;
O bury me not on the lone prairie!

"O bury me not on the lone prairie,
In a narrow grave six foot by three,
Where the buffalo paws o'er a prairie sea;
O bury me not on the lone prairie!

"O bury me not on the lone prairie,
Where the wild coyotes will howl o'er me,
Where the rattlesnakes hiss and the crow flies
    free;
O bury me not on the lone prairie!

"O bury me not," and his voice faltered there,
But we took no heed of his dying prayer;
In a narrow grave just six by three
We buried him there on the lone prairie.

—*Unknown*

*   *   *   *

He is not drunk who, from the floor,
Can rise again and drink some more;
But he is drunk who prostrate lies,
And cannot drink or cannot rise.

—*Thomas Love Peacock*

ROY BEAN

Judge Roy Bean was a fabulous Texan in a state abounding with fabulous characters. He was known as "the law west of the Pecos." This ballad gives a glimpse of his versatility, and proves him to have been indeed a law unto himself.

Cowboys, come and hear a story of Roy Bean in
    all his glory,
"All the law West of the Pecos," was his line:
You must let our ponies take us, to a town on
    Lower Pecos
Where the High Bridge spans the cañon thin
    and fine.

He was born one day near Toyah where he
    learned to be a lawyer
And a teacher and a barber for his fare,
He was cook and old shoe mender, sometimes
    preacher and bar-tender:
It cost two bits to have him cut your hair.

He was certain sure a hustler and considerable
    a rustler
And at mixing up an egg nog he was grand.
He was lively, he was merry, he could drink a
    Tom and Jerry,
On occasion at a round-up took a hand.

You may find the story funny, but once he had
    no money
Which for him was not so very strange and rare,
And he went to help Pap Wyndid but he got so
    absent minded,
That he put his RB brand on old Pap's steer.

108

Now Pap was right smart angry so Roy Bean
  went down to Langtry
Where he opened up an office and a store.
There he'd sell you drinks or buttons or another
  rancher's muttons,
Though the latter made the other feller sore.

Once there came from Austin city a young dude
  reputed witty,
Out of Bean he thought he'd quickly take a rise:
And he got frisky as he up and called for whiskey
And he said to Bean, "Now hurry, damn your
  eyes."

On the counter threw ten dollars and it very
  quickly follers
That the bar-keep took full nine and gave back
  one,
Then the stranger give a holler as he viewed his
  single dollar,
And at that commenced the merriment and fun.

For the dude he slammed the table just as hard
  as he was able,
That the price of whiskey was too high he swore.
Said Roy Bean, "Cause of your fussin' and your
  most outrageous cussin'
You are fined the other dollar by the law.

"On this place I own a lease, sir, I'm the justice
  of the peace, sir,
And the Law west of the Pecos all is here,
For you've acted very badly," then the stranger
  went off sadly
While down his cheek there rolled a bitter tear.

Then one day they found a dead man who had
    been in life a Red man
So it's doubtless he was nothing else than bad.
Called on Bean to view the body, so he took a
    drink of toddy,
Then he listed all the things the dead man had.

Now the find it was quite rare, oh, for he'd been
    a "cocinero"
And his pay day hadn't been so far away,
He'd a bran' new fine white Stetson and a dandy
    Smith and Wesson
And a bag of forty dollars jingled gay.

Said Roy Bean, "You'll learn a lesson for I see
    a Smith and Wesson
And to carry implements of war is wrong,
So I fine you forty dollar," and the man gave
    ne'er a holler
Which concludes this very interesting song.

                                    —*Unknown*

* * * *

JOSHUA EBENEZER FRY

I'm the Constibule of Pumpkinville,
    Jist traded hosses at the mill.
My name's Joshua
    Ebenezer Fry.

I know a thing or two,
    Yew bet yer life I do.
Yew cain't fool me
    'Cause I'm too dern'd sly.

Wal, I swan!
  I must be gittin' on.
Giddap, Napoleon!
  It looks like rain.
I'll shoot a hawk!
  If the critter didn't balk,
I'll lick Jed Hawkins,
  Sure as Joshua's my name.

I went to the County Fair,
  Met a city slicker there.
He says: "Gimme two tens
  Fer a five."
I says: "Ye derned fool,
  I be the Constibule.
Now you're arrested,
  Jist as sure as you're alive."

Wal, I swan!
  I must be gittin' on.
Giddap, Napoleon!
  It looks like rain.
I'll bet two bits
  The money's counterfeit,
That city feller gimme
  Comin' down on the train.

I hitched up the old mare,
  Druv 'er to the County Fair.
Took first prize,
  On a load of squash.
I got so derned full,
  I went and sold the red bull,
And give away the cow
  That wore the silver bell.

111

Wal, I swan!
  I must be gittin' on.
Giddap, Napoleon!
  It looks like rain.
I'll be derned!
  If the butter ain't churned.
Now we'll have some buttermilk,
  Or Josh is not my name.

I got home so derned late,
  Couldn't find the barn gate.
Ma says: "Joshua!
  Is it possible?
Yew air a disgrace.
  Yew ort to go and hide yer face.
I never seed sich actions
  Fer to be a Constibule."

Wal, I swan!
  I must be gittin' on.
Giddap, Napoleon!
  It looks like rain.
I'll be switched,
  And the hay ain't pitched.
Drap in when yew're
  Over to the farm again.

—*Unknown*

★ ★ ★ ★

Poor Martha Snell, she's gone away,
She would if she could, but she could not stay;
She'd two bad legs, and a baddish cough,
But her legs it was that carried her off.

—*Unknown*

THE KID'S LAST FIGHT

The roaring crowds at the ringside always know that every fight might be a kid's last. Death or glory, or a career cutting out paper dolls, awaits them all.

Us two was pals, the Kid and me;
'Twould cut no ice if some gayzee,
As tough as hell, jumped either one,
We'd both light in and hand him some.

Both of a size, the Kid and me,
We tipped the scales at thirty-three;
And when we'd spar 'twas give and take,
I wouldn't slug for any sake.

One day we worked out at the gym,
Some swell guy hangin' round called "Slim"
Watched us and got stuck on the Kid,
Then signed him up, that's what he did.

This guy called "Slim" he owned a string
Of lightweights, welters, everything;
He took the Kid out on the road,
And where they went none of us knowed.

I guess the Kid had changed his name,
And fightin' the best ones in the game.
I used to dream of him at night,
No letters came—he couldn't write.

In just about two months or three
I signed up with Bucktooth McGee.
He got me matched with Denver Brown,
I finished him in half a round.

Next month I fought with Brooklyn Mike,
As tough a boy who hit the pike;
Then Frisco Jim and Battlin' Ben,
And knocked them all inside of ten.

I took 'em all and won each bout,
None of them birds could put me out;
The sportin' writers watched me slug,
Then all the papers run my mug.

"He'd rather fight than eat," they said,
"He's got the punch, he'll knock 'em dead."
There's only one I hadn't met,
That guy they called "The Yorkshire Pet."

He'd cleaned 'em all around in France,
No one in England stood a chance;
And I was champ in U.S.A.,
And knocked 'em cuckoo every day.

Now all McGee and me could think
Was how we'd like to cross the drink,
And knock this bucko for a row,
And grab a wagon load of dough.

At last Mac got me matched all right,
Five thousand smackers for the fight;
Then me and him packed up our grip,
And went to grab that championship.

I done some trainin' and the night
Set for the battle sure was right;
The crowd was wild, for this here bout
Was set to last till one was out.

The mob went crazy when the Pet
Came in, I'd never seen him yet;
And then I climbed up through the ropes,
All full of fight and full of hopes.

The crowd gave me an awful yell,
('Twas even money at the bell)
They stamped their feet and shook the place;
The Pet turned 'round, I saw his face!

My guts went sick, that's what they did,
For Holy Gee, it was the Kid!
We just had time for one good shake,
We meant it, too, it wasn't fake.

Whang! went the bell, the fight was on,
I clinched until the round was gone,
A-beggin', that he'd let me take
The fall for him—he wouldn't fake.

Hell, no, the Kid was on the square,
And said we had to fight it fair,
The crowd had bet their dough on us—
We had to fight (the honest cuss).

The referee was yellin', "Break,"
The crowd was sore and howlin', "Fake."
They'd paid their dough to see a scrap,
And so far we'd not hit a tap.

The second round we both begin.
I caught a fast one on my chin;
And stood like I was in a doze,
Until I got one on the nose.

I started landin' body blows,
He hooked another on my nose,
That riled my fightin' blood like hell,
And we was sluggin' at the bell.

The next round started, from the go
The millin' we did wasn't slow,
I landed hard on him, and then,
He took the count right up to ten.

He took the limit on one knee,
A chance to get his wind and see;
At ten he jumped up like a flash
And on my jaw he hung a smash.

I'm fightin', too, there, toe to toe,
And hittin' harder, blow for blow,
I damn soon knowed he couldn't stay,
He rolled his eyes—you know the way.

The way he staggered made me sick,
I stalled, McGee yelled, "Cop him quick!"
The crowd was wise and yellin', "Fake,"
They'd seen the chance I wouldn't take.

The mob kept tellin' me to land,
And callin' things I couldn't stand;
I stepped in close and smashed his chin,
The kid fell hard; he was all in.

I carried him into his chair,
And tried to bring him to for fair,
I rubbed his wrists, done everything,
A doctor climbed into the ring.

And I was scared as I could be,
The Kid was starin' and couldn't see;
The doctor turned and shook his head;
I looked again—the Kid was dead!

—Unknown

★　★　★　★

UNHAPPY BOSTON

by Paul Revere

Everybody knows Paul Revere for his horsemanship, but few know that he authored "Unhappy Boston," a ballad provoked by the Boston Massacre. It was printed and posted all over the city and aroused the citizens to revolutionary frenzy.

Unhappy Boston! see thy sons deplore
Thy hallowed walks besmear'd with guiltless
      gore.
While faithless Preston and his savage bands,
With murderous rancor stretch their bloody
      hands;
Like fierce barbarians grinning o'er their prey,
Approve the carnage and enjoy the day.
If scalding drops, from rage, from anguish
      wrung,
If speechless sorrows lab'ring for tongue,
Or if a weeping world can aught appease
The plaintive ghosts of victims such as these;
The patriot's copious tears for each are shed,
A glorious tribute which embalms the dead.
But know, Fate summons to that awful goal,
Where justice strips the murderer of his soul:
Should venal C——ts, the scandal of the land,
Snatch the relentless villain from her hand,
Keen execrations on this plate inscrib'd
Shall reach a judge who never can be bribed.

THE BALLAD OF THE OYSTERMAN

by Oliver Wendell Holmes

Dr. Oliver Wendell Holmes managed to be not only one of the greatest physicians of his time, but a humorist who has stood the test of the years.

It was a tall young oysterman lived by the river-
    side,
His shop was just upon the bank, his boat was
    on the tide;
The daughter of a fisherman, that was so straight
    and slim,
Lived over on the other bank, right opposite to
    him.

It was the pensive oysterman that saw a lovely
    maid,
Upon a moonlight evening, a sitting in the
    shade;
He saw her wave her handkerchief, as much as
    if to say,
"I'm wide awake, young oysterman, and all the
    folks away."

Then up arose the oysterman, and to himself
    said he,
"I guess I'll leave the skiff at home, for fear that
    folks should see;
I read it in the story-book, that, for to kiss his
    dear,
Leander swam the Hellespont,—and I will swim
    this here."

And he has leaped into the waves, and crossed
    the shining stream,
And he has clambered up the bank, all in the
    moonlight gleam;
O there were kisses sweet as dew, and words as
    soft as rain,—
But they have heard her father's step, and in he
    leaps again!

Out spoke the ancient fisherman,—"O what was
    that, my daughter?"
" 'Twas nothing but a pebble, sir, I threw into
    the water."
"And what is that, pray tell me, love, that pad-
    dles off so fast?"
"It's nothing but a porpoise, sir, that's been a
    swimming past."

Out spoke the ancient fisherman,—"Now bring
    me my harpoon!
I'll get into my fishing-boat, and fix the fellow
    soon."
Down fell that pretty innocent, as falls a snow-
    white lamb,
Her hair drooped round her pallid cheeks, like
    seaweed on a clam.

Alas for those two loving ones! she waked not
    from her swound,
And he was taken with the cramp, and in the
    waves was drowned;
But Fate has metamorphosed them, in pity of
    their woe,
And now they keep an oyster-shop for mermaids
    down below.

DOT LEEDLE LOWEEZA

by Charles Follen Adams

There was a time when no amateur concert or Sunday evening in the parlor was complete without one German dialect recitation. Adams wrote under the name "Yawcob Strauss," and this particular piece used to have us in stitches.

How dear to dis heart vas mine grandchild,
    Loweeza!
Dot shveet leedle taughter of Yawcob, mine son!
I nefer was tired to hug und to shqveeze her
Vhen home I get back, und der day's vork vas
    done.
Vhen I vas avay, oh, I know dot she miss me,
For vhen I come homevards, she rushes, bell-mell,
Und poots out dot shveet leedle mout' for to kiss
    me
Her "darling oldt gampa," dot she loves so vell.

Katrina, mine frau, she could not do mitoudt her,
She vas sooch a gomfort to her day py day;
Dot shild she make efry von habby aboudt her,
Like sunshine she drife all dheir troubles avay;
She hold der vool yarn vhile Katrina she vind it,
She prings her dot camfire bottle to shmell;
She fetch me mine pipe, too, vhen I don'd can
    find it,
Dot plue-eyed Loweeza dot lofe me so vell.

How shveet, vhen der toils off der veek vas all
    ofer,
Und Sunday vas come, mit its quiet und rest,
To valk mit dot shild 'mong der daisies und
    clofer,
Und look off der leedle birds building dheir nest!

120

Her pright leedle eyes how dhey shparkle mit
    pleasure,
Her laugh it rings oudt shust so clear like a bell;
I dink dhere was nopody haf sooch a treasure
As dot shmall Loweeza dot lofe me so vell.

Vhen vinter vas come, mit its coldt, shtormy
    veddher,
Katrina und I ve musd sit in der house
Und dalk off der bast, by der fireside togeddher,
Or blay mit dot taughter off our Yawcob Strauss.
Oldt age, mit its wrinkles, pegins to remind us
Ve gannot shtay long mid our shildren to dvell;
But soon ve shall meet mit der poys left pehind
    us,
Und dot shveet Loweeza dot lofe us so vell.

★ ★ ★ ★

NOAH AN' JONAH AN'
CAP'N JOHN SMITH

by Don Marquis

I enjoyed appearing in Don Marquis's comedy "Everything's Jake." Don had a gift for expressing profundities in
humorous form, as can readily be seen in "The Old Soak"
and his famous verse about archy and mehitabel. This
ballad is my old friend at his whimsical best and was a
great favorite of Franklin D. Roosevelt.

Noah an' Jonah an' Cap'n John Smith,
Mariners, travelers, magazines of myth,
Settin' up in Heaven, chewin' and a-chawin',
Eatin' their terbaccy, talkin' and a-jawin';
Settin' by a crick, spittin' in the worter,
Talkin' tall an' tactless, as saints hadn't orter,
Lollin' in the shade, baitin' hooks and anglin',
Occasionally friendly, occasionally wranglin'.

121

Noah took his halo from his old bald head
An' swatted of a hoppergrass an' knocked it dead,
An' he baited of his hook, an' he spoke an' said:
"When I was the skipper of the tight leetle Ark
I useter fish fer porpus, useter fish fer shark,
Often I have ketched in a single hour on Monday
Sharks enough to feed the fambly until Sunday—
To feed all the sarpints, the tigers an' donkeys,
To feed all the zebras, the insects an' monkeys,
To feed all the varmints, bears an' gorillars,
To feed all the camels, cats an' armadillers,
To give all the pelicans stews fer their gizzards,
To feed all the owls an' catamounts an' lizards,
To feed all the humans, their babies an' their
    nusses,
To feed all the houn' dawgs an' hippopotamusses,
To feed all the oxens, feed all the asses,
Feed all the bison an' leetle hoppergrasses—
Always I ketched in half an hour on Monday
All that the fambly could gormandize till Sun-
    day!"

Jonah took his harp, to strum an' to string her,
An' Cap'n John Smith tetched his nose with his
    finger.
Cap'n John Smith, he hemmed some and hawed
    some,
An' he bit off a chaw, an' he chewed some an'
    chawed some:—
"When I was to China, when I was to Guinea,
When I was to Javy, an' also in Verginny,
I teached all the natives how to be ambitious,
I learned 'em my trick of ketchin' devilfishes.
I've fitten tigers, I've fitten bears,
I have fitten sarpints an' wolves in their lairs,
I have fit with wild men an' hippopotamusses,
But the periloussest varmints is the bloody octo-
    pusses!

I'd rub my forehead with phosphorescent light
An' plunge into the ocean an' seek 'em out at
    night!
I ketched 'em in grottoes, I ketched 'em in caves,
I used fer to strangle 'em underneath the waves!
When they seen the bright light blazin' on my
    forehead
They used fer to rush at me, screamin' something
    horrid!
Tentacles wavin', teeth white an' gnashin',
Hollerin' an' bellerin', wallerin' an' splashin'!
I useter grab 'em as they rushed from their grots,
Ketch all their legs an' tie 'em into knots!"

Noah looked at Jonah an' said not a word,
But if winks made noises, a wink had been heard.
Jonah took the hook from a mudcat's middle
An' strummed on the strings of his hallelujah
    fiddle;
Jonah gave his whiskers a backhand wipe
An' cut some plug terbaccer an' crammed it in
    his pipe!
—(Noah an' Jonah an' Cap'n John Smith,
Fishermen an' travellers, narratin' myth,
Settin' up in Heaven all eternity,
Fishin' in the shade, contented as could be!
Spittin' their terbaccer in the little shaded creek,
Stoppin' of their yarns fer ter hear the ripples
    speak!
I hope fer Heaven, when I think of this—
You folks bound hellward, a lot of fun you'll
    miss!)
Jonah, he decapitates that mudcat's head,
An' gets his pipe ter drawin'; an' this is what
    he said:
"Excuse me if yer stories don't excite me much!
Excuse me if I seldom agitate fer such!
You think yer fishermen! I won't argue none!

I won't even tell yer the half o' what I done!
You has careers dangerous an' checkered!
All as I will say is: Go an' read my record!
You think yer fishermen! You think yer great!
All I ask is this: Has one of ye been *bait?*
Cap'n Noah, Cap'n John, I heerd when ye hol-
   lered:
What I asks is this: Has one of ye been *swallered?*
It's mighty purty fishin' with little hooks an' reels,
It's mighty easy fishin' with little rods and creels,
It's mighty pleasant ketchin' mudcats fer yer
   dinners,
But here is my challenge fer saints an' fer sinners,
Which one of ye has v'yaged in a varmint's
   inners?
When I see a big fish, tough as Mathooslum,
I used fer to dive into his oozy-goozlum!
When I see a strong fish, wallopin' like a lum-
   micks,
I uster foller 'em, dive into their stummicks!
I could v'yage an' steer 'em, I could understand
   'em,
I uster navigate 'em, I useter land 'em!
Don't you pester *me* with any more narration!
Go git famous! Git a reputation!"

Cap'n John he grinned his hat brim beneath,
Clicked his tongue of silver on his golden teeth;
Noah an' Jonah an' Cap'n John Smith,
Strummin' golden harps, narratin' myth!
Settin' by the shallows forever an' forever,
Swappin' yarns an' fishin' in a little River!

★   ★   ★   ★

Here is a riddle abstruse:
   Canst read the answer right?
Why is it that my tongue grows loose
   Only when I am tight?

—Unknown

124

CASEY AT THE BAT

by Ernest Lawrence Thayer

When Ernest Lawrence Thayer wrote this ballad there was much speculation as to which ball player he was alluding. We Boston boys were resentful, thinking he meant Mike "King" Kelley, the $10,000 Beauty of the Bostons, the highest-priced player up to that time. The famous actor De Wolf Hopper delighted his era with his superb rendition of this masterpiece.

It looked extremely rocky for the Mudville nine
    that day,
The score stood four to six with but an inning
    left to play.
And so, when Cooney died at first, and Burrows
    did the same,
A pallor wreathed the features of the patrons of
    the game.
A straggling few got up to go, leaving there
    the rest,
With that hope which springs eternal within the
    human breast.

For they thought if only Casey could get a whack
    at that,
They'd put up even money with Casey at the
    bat.
But Flynn preceded Casey, and likewise so did
    Blake,
And the former was a pudding and the latter
    was a fake;
So on that stricken multitude a death-like silence
    sat,
For there seemed but little chance of Casey's
    getting to the bat.
But Flynn let drive a single to the wonderment
    of all,
And the much despised Blakey tore the cover off
    the ball,
And when the dust had lifted and they saw what
    had occurred,
There was Blakey safe on second, and Flynn
    a-hugging third.
Then from the gladdened multitude went up a
    joyous yell,
It bounded from the mountain top and rattled
    in the dell,
It struck upon the hillside, and rebounded on
    the flat,
For Casey, mighty Casey, was advancing to the
    bat.
There was ease in Casey's manner as he stepped
    into his place,
There was pride in Casey's bearing and a smile
    on Casey's face,
And when responding to the cheers he lightly
    doffed his hat,
No stranger in the crowd could doubt, 'twas
    Casey at the bat.
Ten thousand eyes were on him as he rubbed his
    hands with dirt,

126

Five thousand tongues applauded as he wiped
    them on his shirt;
And while the writhing pitcher ground the ball
    into his hip—
Defiance gleamed from Casey's eyes—and a sneer
    curled Casey's lip.
And now the leather-covered sphere came hur-
    tling through the air,
And Casey stood a-watching it in haughty
    grandeur there;
Close by the sturdy batsman the ball unheeded
    sped—
"That hain't my style," said Casey—"Strike one,"
    the Umpire said.
From the bleachers black with people there rose
    a sullen roar,
Like the beating of the storm waves on a stern
    and distant shore,
"Kill him! kill the Umpire!" shouted some one
    from the stand—
And it's likely they'd have done it had not Casey
    raised his hand.
With a smile of Christian charity great Casey's
    visage shone,
He stilled the rising tumult and he bade the
    game go on;
He signalled to the pitcher and again the spher-
    oid flew,
But Casey still ignored it and the Umpire said,
    "Strike two."
"Fraud!" yelled the maddened thousands, and
    the echo answered "Fraud."
But one scornful look from Casey and the
    audience was awed;
They saw his face grow stern and cold; they saw
    his muscles strain,
And they knew that Casey would not let that
    ball go by again.

The sneer is gone from Casey's lip; his teeth are
    clenched with hate,
He pounds with cruel violence his bat upon the
    plate;
And now the pitcher holds the ball, and now he
    lets it go,
And now the air is shattered by the force of
    Casey's blow.
Oh! somewhere in this favored land the sun is
    shining bright,
The band is playing somewhere, and somewhere
    hearts are light.
And somewhere men are laughing, and some-
    where children shout;
But there is no joy in Mudville—mighty Casey
    has "Struck Out."

★ ★ ★ ★

THE FROZEN MAID

Charlottie liv'd on a mountain top in a bleak
    and lonely spot,
There were no other dwellings there except her
    father's cot.
And yet, on many a wintry night, young swains
    were gathered there;
Her father kept a social board and she was very
    fair.

On a New Year's Eve as the sun went down, far
    looked her wishful eye
Out from the frosty window pane as a merry
    sleigh dashed by.
At a village fifteen miles away was to be a ball
    that night,
And though the air was piercing cold her heart
    was warm and light.

128

How brightly gleamed her laughing eye, as a well
    known voice she heard;
And dashing up to the cottage door her lover's
    sleigh appeared.
"Oh, daughter dear," her mother cried, "this
    blanket round you fold,
Tonight is a dreadful one, you'll get your death
    of cold."

"Oh, nay, oh, nay!" Charlottie cried, as she
    laughed like a gypsy queen,
"To ride in blankets muffled up I never would
    be seen;
My silken cloak is quite enough, you know 'tis
    lined throughout,
And there's my silken scarf to twine my head
    and neck about."

Her bonnet and her gloves were on, she leaped
    into the sleigh,
And swiftly they sped down the mountain side
    and o'er the hills away.
With muffled beat so silently five miles at length
    were passed,
When Charles with a few and shivering words
    the silence broke at last.

"Such a dreadful night, I never saw, the reins I
    scarce can hold."
Charlottie faintly then replied, "I am exceeding
    cold."
He cracked his whip, he urged his steed much
    faster than before;
And thus five other weary miles in silence were
    passed o'er.

Said Charles: "How fast the shivering ice is
  gathering on my brow,"
And Charlott' then more faintly cried, "I'm
  growing warmer now."
Thus on they rode through frosty air and the
  glittering cold starlight,
Until at last the village lamps and the ballroom
  came in sight.

They reached the door and Charles sprang out,
  he reached his hand to her,
"Why set you there like a monument that has no
  power to stir?"
He called her once, he called her twice, she
  answered not a word;
He asked her for her hands again, but still she
  never stirred.

He took her hand in his,—'twas cold and hard
  as any stone;
He tore the mantle from her face, the cold stars
  o'er it shone.
Then quickly to the lighted hall her lifeless form
  he bore;
Charlottie's eyes had closed for aye, her voice
  was heard no more.

And there he sat down by her side, while bitter
  tears did flow,
And cried, "My own, my charming bride, 'tis
  you may never know."
He twined his arms around her neck, he kissed
  her marble brow;
His thoughts flew back to where she said, "I'm
  growing warmer now."

—*Unknown*

130

THE LETTER EDGED IN BLACK

Oh, he rang the bell and whistled while he
    waited,
And then he said, "Good morning to you, Jack."
But he little knew the sorrow that he brought me
When he handed me a letter edged in black.

CHORUS

As I heard the postman whistling yester morning,
Coming down the pathway with his pack,
Oh, he little knew the sorrow that he brought me
When he handed me that letter edged in black.

With trembling hand I took the letter from him,
I broke the seal and this is what it said:
"Come home, my boy, your dear old father wants
    you!
Come home, my boy, your dear old mother's
    dead!"

CHORUS

I could hear the postman whistling yester
    morning,
Coming down the pathway with his pack,
But he little knew the sorrow that he brought me
When he handed me that letter edged in black.

"The last words that your mother ever uttered—
'Tell my boy I want him to come back,'
My eyes are blurred, my poor old heart is
    breaking,
For I'm writing you this letter edged in black."

I could hear the postman whistling yester morn-
    ing, etc. (CHORUS)

131

I bow my head in sorrow and in silence,
The sunshine of my life it all has fled,
Since the postman brought that letter yester
    morning
Saying, "Come home, my boy, your poor old
    mother's dead!"

I could hear the postman whistling yester morn-
    ing, etc. (CHORUS)

"Those angry words, I wish I'd never spoken,
You know I never meant them, don't you, Jack?
May the angels bear me witness, I am asking
Your forgiveness in this letter edged in black."

I could hear the postman whistling yester morn-
    in, etc. (CHORUS)

—*Unknown*

JOHN MAYNARD

by Horatio Alger, Jr.

Horatio Alger's novels at the start of the century inspired
many a boy to work to become a hero or a millionaire.
This ballad honors the memory of John Maynard, who
gave his life to save others on the burning *Ocean Queen*.

'Twas on Lake Erie's broad expanse
  One bright midsummer day,
The gallant steamer *Ocean Queen*
  Swept proudly on her way.
Bright faces clustered on the deck
  Or leaning o'er the side,
Watched carelessly the feathery foam
  That flecked the rippling tide.

132

Ah, who beneath that cloudless sky,
　　That, smiling, bends serene,
Could dream that danger, awful, vast,
　　Impended o'er the scene—
Could dream that ere an hour had sped
　　That frame of sturdy oak
Would sink beneath the lake's blue waves,
　　Blackened with fire and smoke?

A seaman sought the captain's side,
　　A moment whispered low;
The captain's swarthy face grew pale;
　　He hurried down below.
Alas, too late! Though quick and sharp
　　And clear his orders came,
No human efforts could avail
　　To quench the insidious flame.

The bad news quickly reached the deck,
　　It sped from lip to lip,
And ghastly faces everywhere
　　Looked from the doomed ship.
"Is there no hope, no chance of life?"
　　A hundred lips implore;
"But one," the captain made reply,
　　"To run the ship on shore."

A sailor whose heroic soul
　　That hour should yet reveal,
By name John Maynard, Eastern born,
　　Stood calmly at the wheel.
"Head her southeast!" the captain shouts
　　Above the smothered roar,
"Head her southeast without delay!
　　Make for the nearest shore!"

133

No terror pales the helmsman's cheeks,
  Or clouds his dauntless eye,
As, in a sailor's measured tone,
  His voice responds, "Ay, ay!"
Three hundred souls, the steamer's freight,
  Crowd forward, wild with fear,
While at the stern the dreaded flames
  Above the deck appear.

John Maynard watched the nearing flames,
  But still with steady hand
He grasped the wheel and steadfastly
  He steered the ship to land.
"John Maynard, can you still hold out?"
  He heard the captain cry;
A voice from out the stifling smoke
  Faintly responds, "Ay! ay!"

But half a mile, a hundred hands
  Stretch eagerly to shore;
But half a mile that distance sped,
  Peril shall all be o'er.
But half a mile! Yet stay, the flames
  No longer slowly creep,
But gather round that helmsman bold
  With fierce, impetuous sweep.

"John Maynard!" with an anxious voice
  The captain cries once more.
"Stand by the wheel five minutes yet,
  And we shall reach the shore."
Through flame and smoke that dauntless heart
  Responded firmly still,
Unawed, though face to face with death,
  "With God's good help I will!"

The flames approach with giant strides,
    They scorch his hand and brow;
One arm, disabled, seeks his side,
    Ah! he is conquered now.
But no, his teeth are firmly set,
    He crushes down his pain;
His knee upon the stanchion pressed,
    He guides the ship again.

One moment yet! one moment yet!
    Brave heart, thy task is o'er;
The pebbles grate beneath the keel,
    The steamer touches shore.
Three hundred grateful voices rise
    In praise to God that he
Hath saved them from the fearful fire,
    And from the engulfing sea.

But where is he, the helmsman bold?
    The captain saw him reel;
His nerveless hands released their task;
    He sank beside the wheel.
The wave received his lifeless corpse,
    Blackened with smoke and fire.
God rest him! Never hero had
    A nobler funeral pyre!

★ ★ ★ ★

Here's to the lasses we've loved, my lad,
Here's to the lips we've pressed;
        For of kisses and lasses,
        Like liquor in glasses,
The last is always the best.

—*Unknown*

135

THE LILY OF THE WEST

I just came down from Louisville, some pleasure
    for to find,
A handsome girl from Michigan, so pleasing to
    my mind,
Her rosy cheeks and rolling eyes like arrows
    pierced my breast,
They call her handsome Mary, the Lily of the
    West.

I courted her for many a day, her love I thought
    to gain,
Too soon, too soon she slighted me which caused
    me grief and pain,
She robbed me of my liberty—deprived me of
    my rest,
They call her handsome Mary—the Lily of the
    West.

One evening as I rambled down by yon shady
    grove,
I met a lord of high degree, conversing with
    my love;
He sang, he sang so merrily, whilst I was sore
    oppressed.
He sang for handsome Mary, the Lily of the
    West.

I rushed up to my rival, a dagger in my hand,
I tore him from my true love, and boldly bade
    him stand;
Being mad to desperation, my dagger pierced his
    breast,
I was betrayed by Mary, the Lily of the West.

Now my trial has come on, and sentenced soon
  I'll be,
They put me in the criminal box, and there
  convicted me.
She so deceived the Jury, so modestly did dress,
She far outshone bright Venus, the Lily of the
  West.

Since then I've gained my liberty, I'll rove the
  country through,
I'll travel the city over, to find my loved one
  true,
Although she stole my liberty and deprived me
  of my rest,
Still I love my Mary, the Lily of the West.

—Unknown

★ ★ ★ ★

ROOT HOG OR DIE

I'll tell you a story that happened long ago,
When the English came to America, I s'pose you
  all know,
They couldn't whip the Yankees, I'll tell you
  the reason why,
Uncle Sam made 'em sing Root Hog or Die.

John Bull sent to Boston, as you shall plainly
  see,
Forty large ships loaded clear up with tea,
The Yankees wouldn't pay the tea tax, I'll tell
  you the reason why,
The Yankee boys made 'em sing Root Hog or
  Die.

They first met our armies on the top of Bunker
  Hill,
When it came to fighting I guess they got their
  fill,

137

The Yankee boys chased them off, I'll tell you
    the reason why,
The Yankee boys made 'em sing Root Hog or
    Die.

Then they met our Washington at Yorktown,
There the Yankees mowed 'em down like grass
    from the ground,
Old Cornwallis gave up his sword, I'll tell you
    the reason why,
General Washington made 'em sing Root Hog
    or Die.

Then they came to Baltimore forty years ago,
They tried to take North Point, but found it
    wouldn't go.
The Baltimoreans chased 'em off, I'll tell you
    the reason why,
The Yankee boys made 'em sing Root Hog or
    Die.

Then they marched their armies down to New
    Orleans,
That was the place, I think, that Jackson gave
    'em beans,
They couldn't take our Cotton Bales, I'll tell
    you the reason why,
General Jackson made 'em sing Root Hog or Die.

Now Johnny Bull has been kicking up a fuss,
He'd better keep quiet or he'll surely make it
    worse,
We're bound to have Cuba, I'll tell you the
    reason why,
For Uncle Sam will make 'em sing Root Hog
    or Die.

—Unknown

A POOR UNFORTUNATE

by Frank L. Stanton

I

His hoss went dead an' his mule went lame;
He lost six cows in a poker game;
A harricane came on a summer's day,
An' carried the house whar' he lived away;
Then an airthquake come when they wuz gone,
An' swallered the lan' that the house stood on!
An' the tax collector, *he* come roun'
An' charged him up fer the hole in the groun'!
An' the city marshal—he come in view
An' said he wanted his street tax, too!

II

Did he moan an' sigh? Did he set an' cry
An' cuss the harricane sweepin' by?
Did he grieve that his ol' friends failed to call
When the airthquake come an' swallered all?
Never a word o' blame he said,
With all them troubles on top his head!
Not him . . . He clumb to the top o' the hill—
Whar' standin' room wuz left him still,
An', barin' his head, here's what he said:
"I reckon it's time to git up an' git;
But, Lord, I hain't had the measles yit!"

* * * *

If a task is once begun
Never leave it till it's done.
Be the labor great or small,
Do it well or not at all.

—*Unknown*

FRANKIE AND JOHNNIE

The ballad of Frankie and Johnnie can lay stout claim
to being America's Number One favorite. It has inspired
novels, plays, and motion pictures, perhaps because it deals
with the most basic of human emotions—jealousy. There
are many, many variations of it and it comes in many
lengths. Its parentage is doubtful, but we are quite sure
that while it was born in St. Louis, it grew up all over the
country.

Frankie and Johnnie were lovers,
Oh, Lordy, how they could love;
Swore to be true to each other,
Just as true as the stars above.
  He was her man,
  But he done her wrong.

Frankie, she was a good woman,
Just like everyone knows,
She'd give her man a hundred dollars,
Just to buy himself some clothes.
  He was her man,
  But he done her wrong.

Frankie went to Memphis—
She went on the morning train—
She paid a hundred dollars
For Johnnie a watch and chain.
  He was her man,
  But he done her wrong.

Frankie lived down in a crib-house,
Crib-house with only one door,
Gave all her money to Johnnie,
To throw on the parlor-girls' floor.
  He was her man,
  But he done her wrong.

Johnnie went down to the corner saloon,
He called for a glass of beer;
Frankie went down in an hour or so,
And said, "Has Johnnie Dean been here?"
    He was her man,
    But he done her wrong.

"I'll not tell you any stories,
I'll not tell you a lie,
Johnnie left here about an hour ago
With a girl called Ella Bly."
    He was her man,
    But he done her wrong.

Frankie went down to the pawn-shop,
She bought herself a little forty-four,
She aimed it at the ceiling,
And shot a big hole in the floor.
    He was her man,
    But he done her wrong.

Frankie went down to the hotel,
She rang that hotel bell,
"Stand back, all you floozies,
Or I'll blow you all to hell!"
    He was her man,
    But he done her wrong.

Frankie looked over the transom,
And there before her eye,
Yes, there on the chair sat Johnnie,
Makin' love to Ella Bly.
    He was her man,
    But he done her wrong.

Frankie threw back her kimono,
She took out her bright forty-four,
Root-a-toot-toot, three times she shot,
Right through that hardwood door.
   She shot her man,
   But he done her wrong.

Johnnie he grabbed off his Stetson,
"O-my-gawd, Frankie, don't shoot!"
But Frankie put her finger on the trigger,
And again it went root-a-toot-toot.
   For he was her man,
   But he done her wrong.

"Roll me over once, doctor,
Roll me over slow,
Roll me onto my right side,
For those bullets hurt me so!"
   She finished her man,
   But he done her wrong.

"Bring on your rubber-tired carriages,
Bring on your rubber-tired hack,
Take my daddy to the cemetery,
But bring his suit and wrist-watch back.
   Best part of my man,
   That has done me wrong."

Thirteen girls dressed in mourning,
Thirteen men dressed in black,
They all went out to the cemetery,
But only twelve of the men came back.
   They left her man,
   That had done her wrong.

"Oh, bring 'round a thousand policemen,
Bring 'em around today,
To lock me in the dungeon,
And throw the key away.
  I shot my man,
    But he done me wrong.

"Yes, put me in that dungeon,
Oh, put me in that cell,
Put me where the north wind blows
From the southeast corner of hell.
  I shot my man,
    When he done me wrong."

Frankie then said to the warden,
"What are they goin' to do?"
The warden said to Frankie,
"It's a pardon, my girl, for you.
  You shot your man,
    But he done you wrong."

The sheriff came 'round in the morning,
And said it was all for the best,
He said her lover, Johnnie,
Was nothin' but a gawdam pest.
  He was her man,
    But he done her wrong.

Now it wasn't any kind of murder,
In either the second or third,
This woman simply dropped her lover,
Like a hunter drops a bird.
  He was her man,
    But he done her wrong.

Frankie now sits in the parlor,
Underneath an electric fan,
Telling her little sisters
To beware of the gawdam man.
    They'll do you wrong,
    Yes, they'll do you wrong.

The last time I saw pretty Frankie,
She surely was looking fine,
Diamonds as big as horse birds,
The owner of a big silver mine.
    She was minus her man,
    That had done her wrong.

This story has no moral,
This story has no end,
This story only goes to show
That there ain't no good in men.
    He was her man,
    But he done her wrong.

—*Unknown*

★　★　★　★

A TAKING GIRL

She took my hand in sheltered nooks,
She took my candy and my books,
She took that lustrous wrap of fur,
She took those gloves I bought for her.
She took my words of love and care,
She took my flowers, rich and rare,
She took my time for quite awhile,
She took my kisses, maid so shy—
She took, I must confess, my eye,
She took whatever I would buy.
And then she took another guy.

—*Unknown*

DOWN WENT McGINTY

by Joseph Flynn

"Did you see him?" "Who?" "McGinty." Some of us remember when that was a great joke to pull on the unwary. Joe Flynn used to sing his ballad at the Old Howard theater in Boston and I went in to see him; but I didn't dare tell my mother. The Old Howard is not Carnegie Hall.

Sunday morning just at nine,
Dan McGinty dressed so fine,
Stood looking up at every high stone wall;
When his friend young Pat McCann
Says, "I'll bet five dollars, Dan,
I could carry you to the top without a fall";
So on his shoulders he took Dan;
To climb the ladder he began,
And he soon commenced to reach up near the
    top;
When McGinty, cute old rogue,
To win the five he did let go,
Never thinking just how far he'd have to drop.

CHORUS

Down went McGinty to the bottom of the wall,
And though he won the five, he was more
    dead than alive,
Sure his ribs and nose and back were broke
    from getting such a fall,
Dress'd in his best suit of clothes.

146

From the hospital Mac went home,
When they fix'd his broken bone,
To find he was the father of a child;
So to celebrate it right,
His friend he went to invite,
And he soon was drinking whiskey fast and wild;
Then he waddled down the street
In his Sunday suit so neat
Holding up his head as proud as John the Great;
But in the sidewalk was a hole,
To receive a ton of coal,
That McGinty never saw till just too late.

CHORUS

Down went McGinty to the bottom of the hole,
Then the driver of the cart give the load of
    coal a start,
And it took us half an hour to dig McGinty
    from the coal,
Dress'd in his best suit of clothes.

Now McGinty raved and swore,
About his clothes he felt so sore,
And an oath he took he'd kill the man or die;
So he tightly grabbed his stick
And hit the driver a lick,
Then he raised a little shanty on his eye;
But two policemen saw the muss
And they soon join'd in the fuss,
Then they ran McGinty in for being drunk;
And the Judge says with a smile,
"We will keep you for a while
In a cell to sleep upon a prison bunk."

Down went McGinty to the bottom of the jail,
Where his board would cost him nix, and he
stay'd exactly six,
They were big long months he stopped, for no
one went his bail,
Dress'd in his best suit of clothes.

Now McGinty thin and pale,
One fine day got out of jail,
And with joy to see his boy was nearly wild;
To his home he quickly ran
To meet his wife Bedaley Ann,
But she'd skipped away and took along the child;
Then he gave up in despair,
And he madly pull'd his hair,
As he stood one day upon the river shore,
Knowing well he couldn't swim,
He did foolishly jump in,
Although water he had never took before.

Down went McGinty to the bottom of the bay,
And he must be very wet for they haven't
found him yet,
But they say his ghost comes round the docks
before the break of day,
Dress'd in his best suit of clothes.

★ ★ ★ ★

Here's to wives and sweethearts!
May they never, never meet.

—*Unknown*

BARBARA ALLEN

This is one of the oldest American ballads. But its merit
alone would demand its inclusion here.

In scarlet town, where I was born,
  There was a fair maid dwellin',
Made every youth cry *Well-a-way!*
  Her name was Barbara Allen.

All in the merry month of May
  When green buds they were swellin',
Young Jemmy Grove on his death-bed lay,
  For love of Barbara Allen.

He sent his man in to her then,
  To the town where she was dwellin',
"O haste and come to my master dear,
  If your name be Barbara Allen."

So slowly, slowly rose she up,
  And slowly she came nigh him,
And when she drew the curtain by—
  "Young man, I think you're dyin'."

"O I'm sick and very very sick,
  And it's all for Barbara Allen."
"O the better for me ye'se never be,
  Tho' your heart's blood were a-spillin'!

"O dinna ye mind, young man," says she,
  "When the red wine ye were fillin',
That ye made the healths go round and round,
  And slighted Barbara Allen?"

He turn'd his face unto the wall,
  And death was with him dealin':
"Adieu, adieu, my dear friends all,
  And be kind to Barbara Allen!"

As she was walking o'er the fields,
  She heard the dead-bell knellin';
And every jow the dead-bell gave
  Cried "Woe to Barbara Allen."

"O mother, mother, make my bed,
  O make it saft and narrow:
My love has died for me today,
  I'll die for him tomorrow.

"Farewell," she said, "ye virgins all,
  And shun the fault I fell in;
Henceforth take warning by the fall
  Of cruel Barbara Allen."

                                —*Unknown*

                ★   ★   ★   ★

WAIT FOR THE WAGONS

A hundred thousand Northmen,
  In glittering war array,
Shout, "Onward now to Richmond!
  We'll brook no more delay;
Why give the traitors time and means
  To fortify the way
With stolen guns, in ambuscades?
  Oh! answer us, we pray."

CHORUS OF CHIEFTAINS

          You must wait for the wagons,
          The real army wagons,
          The fat contract wagons,
          Bought in the red-tape way.

Now, if for army wagons,
   Not for compromise you wait,
Just ask them of the farmers
   Of any Union state;
And if you need ten thousand,
   Sound, sound, though second-hand,
You'll find upon the instant
   A supply for your demand.

CHORUS

No! wait for the wagons,
The new army wagons,
The fat contract wagons,
Till the fifteenth of July.

No swindling fat contractors
   Shall block the people's way,
Nor rebel compromisers—
   'Tis treason's reckoning day.
Then shout again our war-cry,
   To Richmond onward move!
We now can crush the traitors,
   And that we mean to prove!

CHORUS

No! wait for the wagons,
The fat contract wagons;
If red-tape so wills it,
Wait till the Judgment-day.

—Unknown

★　★　★　★

God made the world—and rested.
God made man—and rested.
Then God made woman.
Since then, neither God nor man has rested.

—Unknown

151

THE WHORE ON
THE SNOW CRUST

In Defense of Bundling, c. 1786

Northern nights were cold and early Americans much too thrifty to waste fuel, so when the young man came from afar to visit his girl, they bundled. That is, they courted and kept warm in the same bed—with a virtuous pine board between them.

Adam at first was formed of dust,
  As we find of record;
And did receive a wife call'd Eve,
  By a creative word.

From Adam's side a crooked bride,
  We find complete in form;
Ordained that they in bed might lay
  And keep each other warm.

To court indeed they had no need,
  She was his wife at first,
And she was made to be his aid
  Whose origin was dust.

152

Though Adam's wife destroyed his life
  In manner that is awful,
Yet marriage now we all allow
  To be both just and lawful.

And nowadays there is two ways,
  Which of the two is right:
To lie between sheets sweet and clean
  Or sit up all the night.

But some suppose bundling in cloaths
  The good and wise doth vex;
Then let me know which way to go
  To court the fairer sex.

Whether they must be hugg'd and buss'd
  When sitting up all night;
Or whether they in bed may lay,
  Which doth reason invite?

Nature's request is, give me rest,
  Our bodies seek repose;
Night is the time, and 'tis no crime
  To bundle in our cloaths.

Since in a bed a man and maid
  May bundle and be chaste,
It doth no good to burn up wood;
  It is a needless waste.

Let coat and shift be turned adrift,
  And breeches take their flight;
And honest man and virgin can
  Lie quiet all the night;

But if there be dishonesty
  Implanted in the mind,
Breeches nor smocks nor scarce padlocks
  The rage of lust can bind.

Kate, Nance and Sue proved just and true
  Though bundling did practice;
But Ruth beguil'd and proved with child
  Who bundling did despise.

Whores will be whores, and on the floors
  Where many have been laid,
To set and smoke and ashes poke
  Won't keep awake a maid.

Bastards are not at all times got
  In feather beds, we know;
The strumpet's oath convinces both
  Ofttimes it is not so.

One whorish dame I fear to name
  Lest I should give offense,
But in this town she was took down
  Not more than eight months since.

She was the first that on snow crust
  I ever knew to gender;
I'll hint no more about this whore
  For fear I should offend her.

'Twas on the snow when Sol was low
  And was in Capricorn,
A child was got and it will not
  Be long ere it is born.
So unto those that do oppose
  The bundling trade, I say:
Perhaps there's more got on the floor
  Than any other way.

—*Unknown*

LIQUOR & LONGEVITY

The horse and mule live 30 years
And nothing know of wines and beers.
The goat and sheep at 20 die
And never taste of Scotch or Rye.
The cow drinks water by the ton
And at 18 is mostly done.
The dog at 15 cashes in
Without the aid of rum and gin.
The cat in milk and water soaks
And then in 12 short years it croaks.
The modest, sober, bone-dry hen
Lays eggs for nogs, then dies at ten.
All animals are strictly dry:
They sinless live and swiftly die;
But sinful, ginful rum-soaked men
Survive for three score years and ten.
And some of them, a very few,
Stay pickled till they're 92.

—Unknown

★ ★ ★ ★

CAUTION

Saint Patrick was a gentleman
Who through strategy and stealth
Drove all the snakes from Ireland—
Here's a bumper to his health.
But not too many bumpers,
Lest we lose ourselves, and then
Forget the good Saint Patrick
And see the snakes again.

—Unknown

155

WHEN WILLIE WET THE BED

Attributed to Eugene Field

When Willie was a little boy,
   Not more than five or six,
Right constantly he did annoy
   His mother with his tricks,
Yet not a picayune cared I
   For what he did or said,
Unless, as happened frequently,
   The rascal wet the bed.

   Closely he cuddled up to me,
      And put his hands in mine,
   Till all at once I seemed to be
      Afloat in seas of brine,
   Sabean odors clogged the air
      And filled my soul with dread,
   Yet I could only grin and bear
      When Willie wet the bed.

'Tis many times that rascal has
   Soaked all the bed clothes through,
Whereat, I'd feebly light the gas
   And wonder what to do.
Yet there he lay, so peaceful like;
   God bless his curly head;
I quite forgave the little tyke
   For wetting of the bed.

Ah me, those happy days have flown,
　My boy's a father, too,
And little Willies of his own
　Do what he used to do.
And I! Ah, all that's left for me
　Is dreams of pleasures fled;
Our boys ain't what they used to be
　When Willie wet the bed.

Had I my choice, no shapely dame
　Should share my couch with me,
No amorous jade of tarnished fame,
　Nor wench of high degree;
But I should choose and choose again
　The little curly-head
Who cuddled close beside me when
　He used to wet the bed.

★ ★ ★ ★

A PRAYER

Give me work to do;
Give me health;
Give me joy in simple things.
Give me an eye for beauty,
A tongue for truth,
A heart that loves,
A mind that reasons,
A sympathy that understands;
Give me neither malice nor envy,
But a true kindness
And a noble common sense.
At the close of each day
Give me a book,
And a friend with whom
I can be silent.

—Unknown

MADAMOISELLE FROM ARMENTIERS

Madamoiselle from Armentiers, parley voo,
Madamoiselle from Armentiers, parley voo,
    Madamoiselle from Armentiers,
    She hasn't been kissed in forty years,
Hinky, dinky, parley voo.

Madamoiselle from Armentiers, parley voo,
Madamoiselle from Armentiers, parley voo,
    She had a form like the back of a hack,
    When she cried the tears ran down her
      back,
Hinky, dinky, parley voo.

Madamoiselle from Armentiers, parley voo,
Madamoiselle from Armentiers, parley voo,
    She never could hold the love of a man
    'Cause she took her baths in a talcum can,
Hinky, dinky, parley voo.

Madamoiselle from Armentiers, parley voo,
Madamoiselle from Armentiers, parley voo,
    She had four chins, her knees would knock,
    And her face would stop a coo-coo clock,
Hinky, dinky, parley voo.

Madamoiselle from Armentiers, parley voo,
Madamoiselle from Armentiers, parley voo,
    She could guzzle a barrel of sour wine,
    And eat a hog without peeling the rine,
Hinky, dinky, parley voo.

Madamoiselle from Armentiers, parley voo,
Madamoiselle from Armentiers, parley voo,
     She could beg a franc, a drink, a meal,
     But it wasn't because of sex appeal,
Hinky, dinky, parley voo.

The M.P.'s think they won the war, parley voo,
The M.P.'s think they won the war, parley voo,
     The M.P.'s think they won the war
     By standing guard at a café door,
Hinky, dinky, parley voo.

The officers get the pie and cake, parley voo,
The officers get the pie and cake, parley voo,
     The officers get the pie and cake,
     And all we get is the bellyache,
Hinky, dinky, parley voo.

The sergeant ought to take a bath, parley voo,
The sergeant ought to take a bath, parley voo,
     If he ever changes his underwear
     The frogs will give him a croix de guerre,
Hinky, dinky, parley voo.

You might forget the gas and shells, parley voo,
You might forget the gas and shells, parley voo,
     You might forget the groans and yells,
     But you'll never forget the madamoiselles,
Hinky, dinky, parley voo.

Madamoiselle from Armentiers, parley voo,
Madamoiselle from Armentiers, parley voo,
     Just blow your nose and dry your tears
     For we'll be back in a few short years,
Hinky, dinky, parley voo.

                                        —*Unknown*

THE SHOOTING
OF DAN McGREW

by Robert W. Service

Klondike Mike was a famous old sourdough. On his return from the Yukon, the rumor spread that he had been
in at the death of Dan McGrew. Despite his repeated
denials, the rumor persisted until finally Mike began to
believe it himself.

A bunch of the boys were whooping it up in the
     Malamute saloon;
The kid that handles the music-box was hitting
     a jag-time tune;
Back of the bar, in a solo game, sat Dangerous
     Dan McGrew;
And watching his luck was his light-o'-love, the
     lady that's known as Lou.

When out of the night, which was fifty below,
    and into the din and the glare,
There stumbled a miner fresh from the creeks,
    dog-dirty, and loaded for bear.
He looked like a man with a foot in the grave
    and scarcely the strength of a louse,
Yet he tilted a poke of dust on the bar, and he
    called for drinks for the house.
There was none could place the stranger's face,
    though we searched ourselves for a clue;
But we drank his health, and the last to drink
    was Dangerous Dan McGrew.

There's men that somehow just grip your eyes,
    and hold them hard like a spell;
And such was he, and he looked to me like a
    man who had lived in hell;
With a face most hair, and the dreary stare of
    a dog whose day is done,
As he watered the green stuff in his glass, and
    the drops fell one by one.
Then I got to figgering who he was, and wonder-
    ing what he'd do,
And I turned my head—and there watching him
    was the lady that's known as Lou.

His eyes went rubbering round the room, and
    he seemed in a kind of daze,
Till at last that old piano fell in the way of his
    wandering gaze.
The rag-time kid was having a drink: there was
    no one else on the stool,
So the stranger stumbles across the room, and
    flops down there like a fool.
In a buckskin shirt that was glazed with dirt
    he sat, and I saw him sway;
Then he clutched the keys with his talon hands
    —my God! but that man could play.

Were you ever out in the Great Alone, when
    the moon was awful clear,
And the icy mountains hemmed you in with a
    silence you most could *hear*;
With only the howl of a timber wolf, and you
    camped there in the cold,
A half-dead thing in a stark, dead world, clean
    mad for the muck called gold;
While high overhead, green, yellow and red, the
    North Lights swept in bars?—
Then you've a hunch what the music meant . . .
    hunger and night and the stars.

And hunger, not of the belly kind, that's ban-
    ished with bacon and beans,
But the gnawing hunger of lonely men for a
    home and all that it means:
For a fireside far from the cares that are, four
    walls and a roof above,
But oh! so cramful of cozy joy, and crowned
    with a woman's love—
A woman dearer than all the world, and true as
    Heaven is true—
(God! how ghastly she looks through her
    rouge—the lady that's known as Lou.)

Then on a sudden the music changed, so soft
    that you scarce could hear;
But you felt that your life had been looted clean
    of all that it once held dear;
That someone had stolen the woman you loved;
    that her love was a devil's lie;
That your guts were gone, and the best for you
    was to crawl away and die.
'Twas the crowning cry of a heart's despair, and
    it thrilled you through and through—
"I guess I'll make it a spread misere," said
    Dangerous Dan McGrew.

The music almost died away . . . then it burst
    like a pent-up flood;
And it seemed to say, "Repay, repay," and my
    eyes were blind with blood.
The thought came back of an ancient wrong,
    and it stung like a frozen lash,
And the lust awoke to kill, to kill . . . then
    the music stopped with a crash,
And the stranger turned, and his eyes they
    burned in a most peculiar way;
In a buckskin shirt that was glazed with dirt he
    sat, and I saw him sway;
Then his lips went in a kind of grin, and he
    spoke, and his voice was calm,
And "Boys," says he, "you don't know me, and
    none of you care a damn;
But I want to state, and my words are straight,
    and I'll bet my poke they're true,
That one of you is a hound of hell . . . and
    that one is Dan McGrew."

Then I ducked my head, and the lights went out,
    and two guns blazed in the dark,
And a woman screamed, and the lights went up,
    and two men lay stiff and stark.
Pitched on his head, and pumped full of lead,
    was Dangerous Dan McGrew,
While the man from the creeks lay clutched to
    the breast of the lady that's known as Lou.
These are the simple facts of the case, and I
    guess you ought to know.
They say that the stranger was crazed with
    "hooch," and I'm not denying it's so.
I'm not so wise as the lawyer guys, but strictly
    between us two—
The woman that kissed him—and pinched his
    poke—was the lady that's known as Lou.

THE
BOSTON BURGLAR

While the hero of this ballad operated on a scale much smaller than that of our moderns, such as the men who staged the million-dollar Brink holdup in Boston, he did do well enough to get a term in Charlestown jail. Needless to say, like all Bostonians—and some burglars—he came from a respectable family.

I came here from Boston, a town you all know well,
Brought up by honest parents, the truth to you I'll tell.
Brought up by honest parents and raised most tenderly,
Until I started roving, when I was twenty-three.

My character I ruined and I was sent to jail,
My friends they did their levellest to get me out on bail;
The twelve men called me guilty, the clerk he wrote it down.
The judge he passed my sentence, to jail in Charlestown.

They put me on the passenger one cold, cold winter's day.
And every depot that I passed I heard the people say,
"That man's the Boston Burglar, for prison he is bound,
All for his evil doings he's off to Charlestown."

I thought then of my father, a-pleading at the
    bar,
Likewise my patient mother, a-pulling out her
    hair,
A-tearing out her gray locks and tears all stream-
    ing down,
"My darling boy, what have you done to go to
    Charlestown?"

And there's the girl in Boston, the one I love so
    well,
To whom I should be married in peace to live
    and dwell,
When I get out of prison, bad company I'll shun,
I'll never touch another card or look upon bad
    rum.

O people, you in freedom, pray keep so if you
    can,
Remember that it's evil to break the laws of man;
For sad it is to find yourself in such a fix as me,
A-facing twenty-three years in penitentiary.

—Unknown

★ ★ ★ ★

QUATRAIN

by Abraham Lincoln

(Written when a very young man)

> Abraham Lincoln
> His hand and pen
> He will be good but
> God knows when.

165

SWING LOW, SWEET CHARIOT

I looked over Jordan and what did I see,
  Comin' for to carry me home?
A band of angels comin' afteh me,
  Comin' for to carry me home.

CHORUS

Swing low, sweet chariot,
  Comin' for to carry me home;
Swing low, sweet chariot,
  Comin' for to carry me home.

If you get there befo' I do,
  Comin' for to carry me home,
Jus' tell 'em I'm a-comin' too,
  Comin' for to carry me home.   (CHORUS)

I ain't been to heb'n, but I been tol',
  Comin' for to carry me home,
De streets in heb'n am paved wid gol',
  Comin' for to carry me home.   (CHORUS)

I'm sometimes up and sometimes down,
  Comin' for to carry me home;
But still my soul am hebenly-boun',
  Comin' for to carry me home.   (CHORUS)

—*Unknown*

★　★　★　★

I like to hear the rooster crow,
He's like so many men I know,
Who roar and rant and rave and shout
And beat their manly chests, without
A darn thing to brag about.

—*Unknown*

POLLY-WOLLY-DOODLE

Oh, I went down South for to see my Sal,
Sing Polly-wolly-doodle all the day;
My Sally am a spunky girl,
Sing Polly-wolly-doodle all the day.
Fare thee well, fare thee well,
Fare thee well, my fairy fay,
For I'm going to Louisiana
For to see my Susyanna,
Sing Polly-wolly-doodle all the day.

Oh, I came to a river, and I couldn't get across,
Sing Polly-wolly-doodle all the day;
So I jumped on a nigga' an' I thought he was a
    hoss.
Sing Polly-wolly-doodle all the day.

A grasshopper sitting on a railroad track,
Sing Polly-wolly-doodle all the day;
And picking his teeth with a carpet tack,
Sing Polly-wolly-doodle all the day.

Behind the barn down on my knees,
Sing Polly-wolly-doodle all the day,
I think I heard a chicken sneeze,
Sing Polly-wolly-doodle all the day.

He sneezed so hard with the whooping cough,
Sing Polly-wolly-doodle all the day,
He sneezed his head and his tail right off,
Sing Polly-wolly-doodle all the day.

—Unknown

BLACK ROCK PORK

I shipped aboard a lumber-boat,
  Her name was Charles O'Rourke.
The very first thing they rolled aboard
  Was a barrel of Black Rock pork.

They fried a chunk for breakfast
  And a chunk for luncheon too.
It didn't taste so goody-good,
  And it was hard to chew.

From Buffalo to old New York
  They fed it to dear-old-me;
They boiled the barrel and the rest of the pork,
  And we had it all for tea.

About three days out, we struck a rock
  Of Lackawanna coal.
It gave the boat quite a shock,
  And stove in quite a hole.

So I hollered at the driver
  Who was off a-treadin' dirt;
He jumped aboard and stopped the leak
  With his crumby undershirt.

Now the cook upon this canal boat
  Stood six feet in her socks;
She had a bosom like a box-car,
  And her breath would open the locks.

Now the cook is in the poor-house,
  And the crew is all in jail,
And I'm the only canaller
  That is left to tell the tale.

—Unknown

WHEN SOMEONE CARES

When you meet some disappointment,
An' you're feelin' kind-o'-blue;
When your plans have all got sidetracked,
Or some friend has proved untrue;
When you're toilin', prayin', strugglin',
At the bottom of the stairs—
It is like a panacea, just to know that someone
     cares.

It will send a thrill of rapture through the
     framework of the heart;
It will stir the inner bein' till the tear-drops
     want to start;
For this life is worth the livin' when someone
     your sorrow shares—
Life is truly worth the livin' when you know
     that someone cares.

Oh! this world is not all sunshine—some days
     dark clouds disclose;
There's a cross for every joy-bell, an' a thorn for
     every rose;
But the cross is not so grievous, not the thorn
     the rosebud wears—
An' the clouds have silver linin's—when some-
     one really cares.

—Unknown

   ★   ★   ★   ★

How many times we must have met
     Here on the street as strangers do,
Children of chance we were, who passed
     The door of heaven and never knew.

—Unknown

WHAT THE

ENGINES SAID

Opening of the Pacific Railroad, May 12, 1869

by Bret Harte

Bret Harte, who wrote the classic "Outcasts of Poker Flat," caught the spirit of the great railroad era in this fine ballad. That was the era when the states were at last banded together by the great ribbons of steel.

What was it the Engines said,
Pilots touching,—head to head
Facing on the single track,
Half a world behind each back?
This is what the Engines said,
Unreported and unread.

With a prefatory screech,
In a florid Western speech,
Said the Engine from the West:
"I am from Sierra's crest;
And if altitude's a test,
Why, I reckon, it's confessed
That I've done my level best."

Said the Engine from the East:
"They who work best talk the least.
S'pose you whistle down your brakes;
What you've done is no great shakes,—
Pretty fair,—but let our meeting
Be a different kind of greeting.
Let these folks with champagne stuffing,
Not their Engines, do the *puffing*.

"Listen! Where Atlantic beats
Shores of snow and summer heats;
Where the Indian autumn skies
Paint the woods with wampum dyes,—
I have chased the flying sun,
Seeing all he looked upon,
Blessing all that he has blessed,
Nursing in my iron breast
All his vivifying heat,
All his clouds about my crest;
And before my flying feet
Every shadow must retreat."

Said the Western Engine, "Phew!"
And a long, low whistle blew.
"Come, now, really that's the oddest
Talk for one so very modest.
You brag of your East! *You* do?
Why, *I* bring the East to *you*!
All the Orient, all Cathay,
Find through me the shortest way;
And the sun you follow here
Rises in my hemisphere.
Really,—if one must be rude,—
Length, my friend, ain't longitude."

Said the Union: "Don't reflect, or
I'll run over some Director."
Said the Central: "I'm Pacific;
But, when riled, I'm quite terrific.
Yet to-day we shall not quarrel,
Just to show these folks this moral,
How two Engines—in their vision—
Once have met without collision."

This is what the Engines said,
Unreported and unread;
Spoken slightly through the nose,
With a whistle at the close.

* * * *

YOU NEVER MISS THE WATER TILL THE WELL RUNS DRY

When a child I liv'd at Lincoln with my parents
   at the farm,
The lessons that my mother taught to me were
   quite a charm;
She would often take me on her knee when tir'd
   of childish play
And as she pressed me to her breast I've heard
   my mother say:

CHORUS

Waste not, want not, is a maxim I would teach.
Let your watchword be despatch, and practice
   what you preach;
Do not let your chances like sunbeams pass you
   by,
For you never miss the water till the well runs
   dry.

As years roll'd on I grew to be a mischief-making
    boy.
Destruction seem'd my only sport, it was my
    only joy:
And well do I remember when ofttimes well
    chastised,
How father sat beside me then and thus has me
    advised: (CHORUS)

When I arriv'd at manhood I embark'd in
    public life,
And found it was a rugged road, bestrewn with
    care and strife:
I speculated foolishly, my losses were severe,
But still a tiny little voice kept whisp'ring in
    my ear:— (CHORUS)

Then I studied strict economy and found to my
    surprise,
My funds instead of sinking very quickly then
    did rise:
I grasp'd each chance and always struck the iron
    while 'twas hot,
I seiz'd my opportunities and never once forgot:
    (CHORUS)

I'm married now and happy. I've a careful little
    wife.
We live in peace and harmony, devoid of care
    and strife:
Fortune smiles upon us, we have little children
    three.
The lesson that I teach them, as they prattle
    round my knee: (CHORUS)

—Unknown

WHEN JOHNNY COMES MARCHING HOME

by Patrick Sarsfield Gilmore

Besides being the great bandmaster of his time, Patrick Sarsfield Gilmore wrote these stirring words and set them to his equally stirring music.

When Johnny comes marching home again,
  Hurrah! hurrah!
We'll give him a hearty welcome then,
  Hurrah! hurrah!
The men will cheer, the boys will shout,
The ladies, they will all turn out,
  And we'll all feel gay,
When Johnny comes marching home.

The old church-bell will peal with joy,
  Hurrah! hurrah!
To welcome home our darling boy,
  Hurrah! hurrah!
The village lads and lasses say,
With roses they will strew the way;
  And we'll all feel gay,
When Johnny comes marching home.

Get ready for the jubilee,
  Hurrah! hurrah!
We'll give the hero three times three,
  Hurrah! hurrah!
The laurel-wreath is ready now
To place upon his loyal brow,
  And we'll all feel gay,
When Johnny comes marching home.

Let love and friendship on that day,
  Hurrah! hurrah!
Their choicest treasures then display,
  Hurrah! hurrah!
And let each one perform some part,
To fill with joy the warrior's heart;
  And we'll all feel gay,
When Johnny comes marching home.

★ ★ ★ ★

NO MORE BOOZE

There was a little man and he had a little can,
And he used to rush the growler;
He went to the saloon on a Sunday afternoon,
And you ought to hear the bartender holler:

CHORUS

No more booze, no more booze,
No more booze on Sunday;
No more booze, no more booze,
Got to get your can filled Monday.

She's the only girl I love,
With a face like a horse and buggy.
Leaning up against the lake,
O fireman! save my child!

The chambermaid came to my door,
"Get up, you lazy sinner,
We need those sheets for table-cloths
And it's almost time for dinner." (CHORUS)

—*Unknown*

SISTERS OF THE CROSS OF SHAME

by Dana Burnet

What a pleasure it was to meet Dana Burnet at a dinner
party one night and to receive his permission to include
his splendid ballad!

The Sisters of the Cross of Shame,
They smile along the night;
Their houses stand with shuttered souls
And painted eyes of light.

Their houses look with scarlet eyes
Upon a world of sin;
And every man cries, "Woe, alas!"
And every man goes in.

The sober Senate meets at noon,
To pass the Woman's Law,
The churchmen vote to stem
The torrent with a straw.

The Sister of the Cross of Shame,
She smiles beneath her cloud,
(She does not laugh till ten o'clock
And then she laughs too loud).

And still she hears the throb of feet
Upon the scarlet stair,
And still she dons the cloak of shame
That is not hers to wear.

The sons of saintly women come
To kiss the Cross of Shame;
Before them in another time,
Their worthy fathers came.

And no man tells his son the truth,
Lest he should speak of sin;
And every man cries, "Woe, alas!"
And every man goes in.

★   ★   ★   ★

THE NEW COLOSSUS

by Emma Lazarus

The deep feeling of this poem comes from the heart,
for Emma Lazarus was herself a child of the oppressed.
When France presented us with the Statue of Liberty our
officials could not decide what to do with it. For several
years it was left to rust in a vacant lot. Popular subscrip-
tion, spurred by Miss Lazarus, paid for its erection at the
mouth of New York Harbor. There it stands, giving hope
to immigrants from over the sea, and on its base is a part
of this ballad.

Not like the brazen giant of Greek fame,
With conquering limbs astride from land to land,
Here at our sea-washed, sunset gates shall stand
A mighty woman with a torch, whose flame
Is the imprisoned lightning, and her name
Mother of Exiles. From her beacon-hand
Glows world-wide welcome; her mild eyes com-
        mand
The air-bridged harbor that twin cities frame.
"Keep, ancient lands, your storied pomp!" cries
        she
With silent lips. "Give me your tired, your poor,
Your huddled masses yearning to breathe free,
The wretched refuse of your teeming shore.
Send these, the homeless, tempest tossed to me,
I lift my lamp beside the golden door!"

177

THE CREMATION OF SAM McGEE

by Robert W. Service

Mr. Service's admirers are divided as to which is his best
—this or "The Shooting of Dan McGrew." I wonder how
you feel about it.

There are strange things done in the midnight
    sun
  By the men who moil for gold;
The Arctic trails have their secret tales
  That would make your blood run cold;
The Northern Lights have seen queer sights,
  But the queerest they ever did see
Was that night on the marge of Lake Lebarge
  I cremated Sam McGee.

Now Sam McGee was from Tennessee, where the
    cotton blooms and blows.
Why he left his home in the South to roam
    'round the Pole, God only knows.
He was always cold, but the land of gold seemed
    to hold him like a spell;
Though he'd often say in his homely way that
    "he'd sooner live in hell."

On a Christmas Day we were mushing our way
    over the Dawson trail.
Talk of your cold! through the parka's fold it
    stabbed like a driven nail.
If our eyes we'd close, then the lashes froze till
    sometimes we couldn't see;
It wasn't much fun, but the only one to whimper
    was Sam McGee.

And that very night, as we lay packed tight in
    our robes beneath the snow,
And the dogs were fed, and the stars o'erhead
    were dancing heel and toe,
He turned to me, and "Cap," says he, "I'll cash
    in this trip, I guess;
And if I do, I'm asking that you won't refuse
    my last request."

Well, he seemed so low that I couldn't say no;
    then he says with a sort of moan:
"It's the cursed cold, and it's got right hold till
    I'm chilled clean through to the bone.
Yet 'tain't being dead—it's my awful dread of
    the icy grave that pains;
So I want you to swear that, foul or fair, you'll
    cremate my last remains."

A pal's last need is a thing to heed, so I swore I
    would not fail;
And we started on at the streak of dawn; but
    God! he looked ghastly pale.
He crouched on the sleigh, and he raved all day
    of his home in Tennessee;
And before nightfall a corpse was all that was
    left of Sam McGee.

With a corpse half hid that I couldn't get rid, I
    hurried, horror-driven,
There wasn't a breath in that land of death, and
    because of a promise given;
It was lashed to the sleigh, and it seemed to say:
    "You may tax your brawn and brains,
But you promised true, and it's up to you to
    cremate those last remains."

Now a promise made is a debt unpaid, and the
    trail has its own stern code.
In the days to come, though my lips were dumb,
    in my heart how I cursed that load.
In the long, long night, by the lone firelight,
    while the huskies, round in a ring,
Howled out their woes to the homeless snows—
    O God! how I loathed the thing.

And every day that quiet clay seemed to heavy
    and heavier grow;
And on I went, though the dogs were spent and
    the grub was getting low;
The trail was bad, and I felt half mad, but I
    swore I would not give in;
And I'd often sing to the hateful thing, and it
    harkened with a grin.

Till I came to the marge of Lake Lebarge, and
    a derelict there lay;
It was jammed in the ice, but I saw in a trice
    it was called the "Alice May."
And I looked at it, and I thought a bit, and I
    looked at my frozen chum;
Then "Here," said I, with a sudden cry, "is my
    cre-ma-tor-eum."

Some planks I tore from the cabin floor, and I
    lit the boiler fire;
Some coal I found that was lying around, and
    I heaped the fuel higher;
The flames just roared, and the furnace roared—
    such a blaze you seldom see;
And I burrowed a hole in the glowing coal, and
    I stuffed in Sam McGee.

Then I made a hike, for I didn't like to hear
    him sizzle so;
And the heavens scowled, and the huskies
    howled, and the wind began to blow.
It was icy cold, but the hot sweat rolled down my
    cheeks, and I don't know why;
And the greasy smoke in an inky cloak went
    streaking down the sky.

I do not know how long in the snow I wrestled
    with grisly fear;
But the stars came out and they danced about
    ere again I ventured near;
I was sick with dread, but I bravely said: "I'll
    just take a peep inside.
I guess he's cooked, and it's time I looked";
    . . . then the door I opened wide.

And there sat Sam, looking cool and calm, in
    the heart of the furnace roar;
And he wore a smile you could see a mile, and he
    said: "Please close that door.
It's fine in here, but I greatly fear you'll let in
    the cold and storm—
Since I left Plumtree, down in Tennessee, it's the
    first time I've been warm."

*There are strange things done in the midnight
    sun*
  By the men who moil for gold;
The Arctic trails have their secret tales
  That would make your blood run cold;
The Northern Lights have seen queer sights,
  But the queerest they ever did see
Was that night on the marge of Lake Lebarge
 I cremated Sam McGee.

★   ★   ★   ★

WHAT ONE MAY AND MAY NOT CALL A WOMAN

You may call a woman a kitten, but you must
    not call her a cat.
You may call her a mouse, but you must not
    call her a rat.
You may call her a chicken, but you must not
    call her a hen.
You may call her a duck, but you must not
    call her a goose.
You may call her a vision, but you must not
    call her a sight.

—Unknown

THE OREGON TRAIL

Away down yonder in the Wahee Mountains,
Where folks don't know about books nor count-
   in's,
There lived a Zeke, an old galoot,
And all he knew was how to shoot.
He had a girl and he would always tell 'er
Not to monkey with a city feller;
The city feller came without fail
And old Zeke shot him on the Oregon Trail.

On the Oregon Trail, that's where he shot 'im;
On the Oregon Trail, they came down and got
   'im.
The city feller came without fail
And old Zeke shot 'im on the Oregon Trail.

Hezekiah.had a lovely daughter,
Never did a thing she hadn't oughter,
She married Zeke and they went alone
Up in the mountains and built a home.
It wasn't long until the stork came flying,
Brought a kid that was always crying.
The poor stork died he grew so frail—
Couldn't stand it on the Oregon Trail.

On the Oregon Trail, that's where they killed
   'im.
On the Oregon Trail a tomb they built 'im.
They dug his grave and on it wrote:
"This poor bird was the family goat."
He carried kids until his back was broke on the
   Oregon Trail.

—Unknown

THE DARK GIRL
DRESSED IN BLUE

'Twas on a Friday morning,
  The first day of August;
When of that day I ever think,
  My heart feels ready to bust!
I jumped into a Broadway stage,
  The Central Park going to.
On a seat by the right-hand side of the door,
  Sat a dark girl dressed in blue.

Now we hadn't gone very far,
  When the lady looked so strange;
The driver knocked down for his fare,
  Says she, "I have no change;
I've only a ten-dollar bill,
  O dear, what shall I do?"
Said I, "Allow me to pay." "O, thank you, sir,"
  Says the dark girl dressed in blue.

We chatted and talked as we onward walked,
  About one thing or the other;
She asked me, too (O wasn't it kind?),
  If I had a father or a mother.
Says I, "Yes, and grandmother, too;
  But pray, miss, what are you?"
"O, I'm chief engineer in a milliner's shop,"
  Says the dark girl dressed in blue.

We walked about for an hour or two,
  Through the park, both near and far;
Then to a large hotel we went—
  I stepped up to the bar;
She slipped in my hand a ten-dollar bill.
  I said, "What are you going to do?"
"O, don't think it strange, I must have change,"
  Said the dark girl dressed in blue.

We had some slight refreshments,
   And I handed out the bill;
The bar-keep counted out the change,
   And the bill dropped in the till:
'Twas in currency and silver change;
   There was a three-cent piece or two;
So I rolled it up, and gave it to
   The dark girl dressed in blue.

She thanked me, and said, "I must away;
   Farewell, till next we meet;
For on urgent business I must go
   To the store in Hudson Street."
She quickly glided from my sight,
   And soon was lost to view;
I turned to leave—when by my side
   Stood a tall man dressed in blue!

This tall man said, "Excuse me, sir,
   I'm one of the 'special force';
That bill was bad—please come with me"—
   I had to go, of course.
Said I, "For a lady I obtained the change."
   Says he, "Are you telling me true?
What's her name?" Says I, "I don't know,
   She was a dark girl dressed in blue."

My story they believed—thought I was deceived,
   But said I must hand back the cash;
I thought it was a sin, as I gave her the tin—
   Away went ten dollars smash!
So, all young men, take my advice,
   Be careful what you do,
When you make the acquaintance of ladies
     strange,
   Especially a dark girl dressed in blue.

—Unknown

THE FALL OF TECUMSEH

October 5, 1813

What heavy-hoofed coursers the wilderness
  roam,
  To the war-blast indignantly tramping?
Their mouths are all white, as if frosted with
  foam,
  The steel bit impatiently champing.

'Tis the hand of the mighty that grasps the rein.
  Conducting the free and the fearless.
Ah! See them rush forward, with wild disdain,
  Through paths unfrequented and cheerless.

From the mountains had echoed the charge of
  death,
  Announcing that chivalrous sally;
The savage was heard, with untrembling breath,
  To pour his response from tho valley.

One moment, and nought but the bugle was
  heard,
  And nought but the war-whoop given;
The next, and the sky seemed convulsively
  stirred,
  As if by the lightning riven.

The din of the steed, and the sabred stroke,
  The blood-stifled gasp of the dying,
Were screened by the curling sulphur-smoke,
  That upward went wildly flying.

In the mist that hung over the field of blood,
  The chief of the horsemen contended;
His rowels were bathed in purple flood,
  That fast from his charger descended.

That steed reeled, and fell, in the van of the
 fight.
  But the rider repressed not his daring,
Till met by a savage, whose rank and might
  Were shown by the plume he was wearing.

The moment was fearful; a mightier foe
  Had ne'er swung the battle-axe o'er him;
But hope nerved his arm for a desperate blow,
  And Tecumseh fell prostrate before him.

O ne'er may the nations again be cursed
  With the conflict so dark and appalling!—
Foe grappled with foe, till the life-blood burst
  From their agonized bosoms in falling.

Gloom, silence, and solitude rest on the spot
  Where the hopes of the red man perished;
But the fame of the hero who fell shall not,
  By the virtuous, cease to be cherished.

He fought, in defence of his kindred and king,
  With a spirit most loving and loyal.
And long shall the Indian warrior sing
  The deeds of Tecumseh the royal.

The lightning of intellect flashed from his eye,
  In his arm slept the force of the thunder,
But the bolt passed the suppliant harmlessly by,
  And left the freed captive to wonder.

Above, near the path of the pilgrim, he sleeps,
  With a rudely built tumulus o'er him;
And the bright-bosomed Thames, in his majesty,
  sweeps,
  By the mound where his followers bore him.

                              —*Unknown*

SAM HALL

There is an expression of defiance in this ballad worthy of any great rogue or hero in the history of mankind. Read it over and feel your blood tingling in your veins.

Oh, my name it is Sam Hall, it is Sam Hall;
Yes, my name it is Sam Hall, it is Sam Hall;
Yes, my name it is Sam Hall, and I hate you one
and all,
Yes, I hate you one and all, God damn your eyes.

Oh, I killed a man, they say, so they say;
Yes, I killed a man, they say, so they say;
I beat him on the head, and I left him there for
dead,
Yes, I left him there for dead, God damn his eyes.

188

Oh, the parson he did come, he did come;
Yes, the parson he did come, he did come;
And he looked so bloody glum, as he talked of
    Kingdom Come—
He can kiss my ruddy bum, God damn his eyes.

And the sheriff he came too, he came too;
Yes, the sheriff he came too, he came too;
Yes, the sheriff he came too, with his men all
    dressed in blue—
Lord, they were a bloody crew, God damn their
    eyes.

Now up the rope I go, up I go;
Yes, up the rope I go, up I go;
And those bastards down below, they'll say,
    "Sam, we told you so,"
They'll say, "Sam, we told you so," God damn
    their eyes.

I saw my Nellie dressed in blue, dressed in blue;
I saw my Nellie in the crowd, all dressed in blue,
Says my Nellie, dressed in blue, "Your trifling
    days are through—
Now I know that you'll be true, God damn your
    eyes."

And now in heaven I dwell, in heaven I dwell;
Yes, now in heaven I dwell, in heaven I dwell;
Yes, now in heaven I dwell—Holy Christ; it is a
    sell—
All the whores are down in hell, God damn their
    eyes.

                                    —*Unknown*

THE BATTLE OF EUTAW

September 8, 1781

by William Gilmore Simms

In the ante-bellum days anyone who wrote for a living was held in low esteem by the elite of Charleston, S.C., but a respectable merchant or professional man might woo the muse with approval. One of these, William Gilmore Simms, was a lawyer, but we doubt if his legal triumphs ever outshone "The Battle of Eutaw."

Hark! 'tis the voice of the mountain,
   And it speaks to our heart in its pride,
As it tells of the bearing of heroes
   Who compassed its summits and died!
How they gathered to strife as the eagles,
   When the foeman had clambered the height!
How, with scent keen and eager as beagles,
   They hunted him down for the fight.

Hark! through the gorge of the valley,
   'Tis the bugle that tells of the foe;
Our own quickly sounds for the rally,
   And we snatch down the rifle and go.
As the hunter who hears of the panther,
   Each arms him and leaps to his steed,
Rides forth through the desolate antre,
   With his knife and his rifle at need.

From a thousand deep gorges they gather,
   From the cot lowly perched by the rill,
The cabin half hid in the heather,
   'Neath the crag which the eagle keeps still;
Each lonely at first in his roaming,
   Till the vale to the sight opens fair,
And he sees the low cot through the gloaming,
   When his bugle gives tongue to the air.

190

Thus a thousand brave hunters assemble
    For the hunt of the insolent foe,
And soon shall his myrmidons tremble
    'Neath the shock of the thunderbolt's blow.
Down the lone heights now wind they together,
    As the mountain-brooks flow to the vale,
And now, as they group on the heather,
    The keen scout delivers his tale:

"The British—the Tories are on us,
    And now is the moment to prove
To the women whose virtues have won us,
    That our virtues are worthy their love!
They have swept the vast valleys below us
    With fire, to the hills from the sea;
And here would they seek to o'erthrow us
    In a realm which our eagle makes free!"

No war-council suffered to trifle
    With the hours devote to the deed;
Swift followed the grasp of the rifle,
    Swift followed the bound to the steed;
And soon, to the eyes of our yeomen,
    All panting with rage at the sight,
Gleamed the long wavy tents of the foeman,
    As he lay in his camp on the height.

Grim dashed they away as they bounded,
    The hunters to hem in the prey,
And, with Deckard's long rifles surrounded,
    Then the British rose fast to the fray;
And never with arms of more vigor
    Did their bayonets press through the strife,
Where, with every swift pull of the trigger,
    The sharpshooters dashed out a life!

'Twas the meeting of eagles and lions;
 'Twas the rushing of tempests and waves;
Insolent triumph 'gainst patriot defiance,
 Born freemen 'gainst sycophant slaves;
Scotch Ferguson sounding his whistle,
 As from danger to danger he flies,
Feels the moral that lies in Scotch thistle,
With its "touch me who dare!" and he dies!

An hour, and the battle is over;
 The eagles are rending the prey;
The serpents seek flight into cover,
 But the terror still stands in the way:
More dreadful than doom that on treason
 Avenges the wrongs of the state;
And the oak-tree for many a season
 Bears fruit for vultures of fate!

★ ★ ★ ★

A DRUNKARD'S ODE

How well do I remember, 'twas in the late
 November,
 I was walking down the street quite full of
 pride,
My heart was all a-flutter as I slipped down in
 the gutter,
 And a pig came there and laid down by my
 side;
And as I lay there in the gutter, all too soused to
 even mutter,
 A lady passing by was heard to say:
"One may tell a brute that boozes by the
 company he chooses."
 Hearing this the pig got up and walked away.

—*Unknown*

RACKETTY JACK

My cognomen is Racketty Jack,
   A noisy swell am I,
I care not how the world may sway,
   I never will say die;
In grog and beer I do indulge,
   Sometimes in cliquot too,
A bottle of "phizz" is all my eye,
   Bring in a dozen or two.

CHORUS

Hi! ho! ho! stop!
Here, waiter, brandy hot!
I'm Racketty Jack, no money I lack,
And I'm the boy for a spree.

When I go out at night, my boys,
   I'm always ripe for fun,
And amongst the fair, I do declare,
   I always was "A 1."
Though a harum-scarum sort of chap,
   I ne'er forget the gals,
For next to them, there's nothing on earth
   Like phizz and jolly good pals. (CHORUS)

I like a lark, I do of course,
   I can't help being gay,
I follow in my father's steps,
   So at least the people say;
For beauty I admire,
   For a spree I'm always fresh,
You see what's bred in the bone, my boys,
   Is sure to come out in the flesh. (CHORUS)

I never fall out with a policeman,
    Nor cheat a hackman's fare,
Nor, like low swells, wrench knockers off,
    And kick stalls in the air;
For I can true enjoyment find,
    With friends like you at my back,
So enjoy yourselves as long as you can,
    And hurrah for Racketty Jack. (CHORUS)

—*Unknown*

* * * *

OUT OF THE TAVERN

Out of the tavern I've just stepped to-night,
Street, you are caught in a very bad plight;
Right hand and left hand are both out of place,
Street, you are drunk, it's a very clear case.

Moon, 'tis a very queer figure you cut,
One eye is staring while the other is shut,
Tipsy, I see, and you're greatly to blame,
Old as you are, 'tis a terrible shame.

And now the street lamp—what a scandalous
    sight,
None of them soberly standing upright,
Rocking and swaggering—why, on my word,
Each of the lamps is as drunk as a lord.

All is confusion—now isn't it odd,
I am the only thing sober abroad;
It would be rash with the crew to remain,
Better go back to the tavern again.

—*Unknown*

THE ROLLING STONE

by Will Thomas Withrow

I'm an A-1 charter member
Of the Ramblers of Unrest,
Known to every bird of passage,
From Chicago to Key West.

I have preached in Kansas City,
Sold insurance in St. Paul,
Peddled books in Dallas, Texas,
And went hungry in them all;
I have ballyhooed with circuses,
Throughout the Middle West,
Done the county fairs in Georgia,
Been the city jailer's guest;
I have harvested in Kansas,
Cooked for lumber camps in Maine,
Gathered fruit in California,
In the sunshine and the rain;
I have been a "cub" reporter,
On full many a small-town sheet,
I have run an all-night lunch stand,
Sold cheap gimcracks on the street;
I have ridden rods and bumpers,
From Seattle to New York,
Crossed the seas to chase adventure—
Paris, Berlin, Dublin, Cork;
I have bummed my way through China,
Stowed away, across the sea,
Mooched my eats through half of Europe,
Mostly broke but always free.
Travelled some? Well, pard, I'll say so!
But I also rise to say
That I've found no place that suits me
Like the good old U.S.A.!

LIPS THAT TOUCH LIQUOR

by George W. Young

To kiss a young lady when you had liquor on your breath was considered highly improper in my young days. I have reason to know this. But along came Prohibition, bringing what Heywood Broun called "coeducational drinking."

You are coming to woo me, but not as of yore,
When I hastened to welcome your ring at the
    door;
For I trusted that he who stood waiting me then
Was the brightest, the truest, the noblest of men.
Your lips on my own when they printed "Fare-
    well"
Had never been soiled by the "beverage of Hell,"
But they come to me now with the bacchanal
    sign,
And the lips that touch liquor must never touch
    mine.

I think of that night in the garden alone,
When in whispers you told me your heart was
my own,
That your love in the future should faithfully be
Unshared by another, kept only for me.
Oh, sweet to my soul is the memory still
Of the lips which met mine, when they whis-
pered "I will";
But now to their pressure they no more incline,
For the lips that touch liquor must never touch
mine.

Oh, John! how it crushed me, when first in your
face
The pen of the "Rum Fiend" had written "dis-
grace";
And turned me in silence and tears from that
breath
All poisoned and foul from the chalice of death.
It scattered the hopes I had treasured to last;
It darkened the future and clouded the past;
It shattered my idol, and ruined the shrine,
For the lips that touch liquor must never touch
mine.

I loved you—Oh, dearer than language can tell,
And you saw it, you proved, you knew it too well!
But the man of my love was far other than he
Who now from the "Tap-room" comes reeling
to me;
In manhood and honor so noble and right—
His heart was so true, and his genius so bright—
And his soul was unstained, unpolluted by wine;
But the lips that touch liquor must never touch
mine.

You promised reform, but I trusted in vain;
Your pledge was but made to be broken again;
And the lover so false to his promises now,
Will not as a husband be true to his vow.
The word must be spoken that bids you depart—
Though the effort to speak it should shatter my
    heart—
Though in silence, with blighted affection, I
    pine,
Yet the lips that touch liquor must never touch
    mine!

If one spark in your bosom of virtue remain,
Go fan it with prayer till it kindles again;
Resolved, with "God helping," in future to be
From wine and its follies unshackled and free!
And when you have conquered this foe of your
    soul—
In manhood and honor beyond his control—
This heart will again beat responsive to thine,
And the lips free from liquor be welcome to
    mine.

*   *   *   *

DUTY

by Edwin Markham

When Duty comes a-knocking at your gate,
Welcome him in; for if you bid him wait,
He will depart only to come once more
And bring seven other duties to your door.

198

BATTLE-HYMN OF THE REPUBLIC

by Julia Ward Howe

Mine eyes have seen the glory of the coming of
the Lord;
He is trampling out the vintage where the
grapes of wrath are stored;
He hath loosed the fateful lightning of his terrible swift sword:
His truth is marching on.

I have seen him in the watch-fires of a hundred
circling camps;
They have builded him an altar in the evening
dews and damps;
I can read his righteous sentence by the dim
and flaring lamps:
His day is marching on.

I have read a fiery gospel, writ in burnished
rows of steel:
"As ye deal with my condemners, so with you
my grace shall deal;
Let the Hero, born of woman, crush the serpent
with his heel,
Since God is marching on."

He has sounded forth the trumpet that shall
never call retreat;
He is sifting out the hearts of men before his
judgment-seat:
O, be swift, my soul, to answer him! be jubilant,
my feet!
Our God is marching on.

In the beauty of the lilies Christ was born across
    the sea,
With a glory in his bosom that transfigures you
    and me;
As he died to make men holy, let us die to make
    men free,
    While God is marching on.

He is coming like the glory of the morning on
    the wave,
He is wisdom to the mighty, he is honor to the
    brave,
So the world shall be his footstool, and the soul
    of wrong his slave,
    Our God is marching on!

* * * *

SHE PLAYS THE GAME

She plays the game with a ready hand,
A steady hand and true;
She marked her man when the game began
And she knows him through and through.
Nothing to win and nothing to lose,
And nothing to choose or care—
A kiss for the stakes, and, if his heart breaks,
She is only playing fair.
A smile, a rose and a maddened fool,
A saddened fool and wise—
The game is done, the woman won—
Dear God! the look in her eyes!
But, ah, time was e'er the woman would,
E'er the woman could, and now
She owes her skill to the careless will
Of the man who taught her how!

—*Unknown*

A FIREMAN'S LIFE

At 2:00 A.M. the station bell
    Rang fit to wake the dead.
Said Pat, "A fireman's life is hell,"
    As he jumped out of bed.

He tucked his jammers in his boots
    And kissed the captain's daughter,
And then the truck went shoot-the-shutes
    To give the fire some water.

Before the burning block they came
    And in a window high
A slowly roasting, toasting dame
    Caught Paddy's eagle eye.

She was a peach, a luscious peach,
    But nearly canned for good,
As she began to moan and screech
    At Paddy where he stood.

So Paddy swung a ladder fast
    And soon was by her side.
"Be brave." he said, "the danger's past,
    To safety we will glide."

He bore her fondly in his arms,
    All snug and highty-tighty,
Because the gown for fire-alarms
    Is nothing but a nighty.

And when he got her safe below,
    And laid her on the ground,
She clung to him and said, "Don't go—
    I like to have you 'round."

So then he tried to calm her heart,
   But she grew hot and hotter.
Said Pat, "This fireman's life's the part
   For me, or else I am a rotter."

"Hot lips," he said, "must have first aid,
   And that is where I shine."
"You do," replied the rescued maid,
   "For yours are hot as mine."

And when at last the blaze was out
   The captain called the roll,
And Paddy answered with a shout,
   "The fire's beyond control!"

—Unknown

* * * *

THE OLD OAKEN BUCKET

by Samuel Woodworth

Paradoxically enough, this piece extolling the virtues of water as a beverage originated in a barroom. Mr. Samuel Woodworth, a New York printer, finished his brandy at Mr. Mallory's bar and commended it over all other drinks. Mr. Mallory replied, "No, you're mistaken. There's a drink surpassing all others—fresh water from the old oaken bucket that hung in the well." After a wistful pause, tears came to Mr. Woodworth's eyes as he softly murmured, "Very true." He had another brandy to think about it.

How dear to this heart are the scenes of my
   childhood,
When fond recollections present them to view!—
The orchard, the meadow, the deep-tangled
   wildwood,
And every loved spot which my infancy knew!

The wide-spreading pond, and the mill that
    stood by it;
The bridge, and the rock where the cataract fell;
The cot of my father, the dairy-house nigh it;
An e'en the rude bucket that hung in the
    well,—
The old oaken bucket, the iron-bound bucket,
The moss-covered bucket which hung in the
    well.

That moss-covered vessel I hailed as a treasure;
For often at noon, when returned from the field,
I found it the source of an exquisite pleasure,—
The purest and sweetest that nature can yield.
How ardent I seized it, with hands that were
    glowing,
And quick to the white-pebbled bottom it fell!
Then soon, with the emblem of truth over-
    flowing,
And dripping with coolness, it rose from the
    well,—
The old oaken bucket, the iron-bound bucket,
The moss-covered bucket arose from the well.

How sweet from the green, mossy brim to receive
    it,
As, poised on the curb, it inclined to my lips!
Not a full, blushing goblet could tempt me to
    leave it,
The brightest that beauty or revelry sips.
And now, far removed from the loved habita-
    tion,
The tear of regret will intrusively swell,
As fancy reverts to my father's plantation,
And sighs for the bucket that hangs in the
    well,—
The old oaken bucket, the iron-bound bucket,
The moss-covered bucket that hangs in the well.

OH, MY DARLING CLEMENTINE

This ballad is in the mood of Stephen Foster and has been erroneously attributed to him. I have never found the true author.

In a cavern, in a canyon,
Excavating for a mine,
Dwelt a miner, 'Forty-Niner,
And his daughter Clementine.

CHORUS

Oh, my darling, oh, my darling,
Oh, my darling Clementine,
You are lost and gone forever,
Dreadful sorry, Clementine.

Light she was and like a fairy,
And her shoes were number nine;
Herring boxes, without topses,
Sandals were for Clementine.   (CHORUS)

Drove she ducklings to the water,
Every morning just at nine;
Hit her foot against a splinter,
Fell into the foaming brine.   (CHORUS)

Ruby lips above the water,
Blowing bubbles soft and fine;
Alas for me! I was no swimmer,
So I lost my Clementine.   (CHORUS)

In a churchyard, near the canyon,
Where the myrtle doth entwine,
There grow roses and other posies,
Fertilized by Clementine.   (CHORUS)

Then the miner, 'Forty-Niner,
Soon began to peak and pine,
Thought he oughter jine his daughter,
Now he's with his Clementine.   (CHORUS)

In my dreams she still doth haunt me,
Robed in garments soaked in brine,
Though in life I used to hug her,
Now she's dead, I'll draw the line.   (CHORUS)

—*Unknown*

* * * *

A MOTHER'S NAME

No painter's brush nor poet's pen
    In justice to her fame
Has ever reached half high enough
    To write a mother's name.

—*Unknown*

THE OLD, OLD STORY

You say I've no place among women,
  You call me a girl of the town.
Well, I am; but I'm what the world made me,
  It is no fault of mine that I'm down.
Your path perhaps was scattered with roses,
  The camellias o'ershadowed my door,
Yet I once had a good and fond mother,
  But our misfortune was we were poor.

Poor and lonely, for years we were honest,
  And worked hard for rent and for bread;
I say we—I mean mother and I—
  For father had long since been dead.
Poor mother, she took in shirt-making,
  For which little enough they would pay,
I clerked in a store for a pittance
  For ten long hours each day.

Girls said that I'd soon catch a lover
  Who would pay for a beautiful wife;
Well, I found one, and he is the cause
  Of my leading a dissolute life.
He was handsome enough as a man goes,
  And his money he spent like a lord;
I gave up my lips to his kisses,
  But of marriage he seldom spoke word.

He told me the days of fond wooing,
  Were always the hey-days of life,
And that when he could claim his large fortune
  'Twould be time for to cherish a wife.
I took all his protests as gospel,
  And gave him my heart in return;
I had scarcely then seen sixteen summers,
  And since found I had plenty to learn.

For a year I was supremely happy,
  The only care that would shadow my brow
Was the thought that perchance I might lose
    him
  He was dearer than life to me now.
I lived on his words and his kisses;
  When his strong arm encircled my waist
The hot blood would rush up to my temples
  And banish all thoughts that were chaste.

Well, the winter was long and a hard one,
  I was rugged and could stand the cold blast,
But poor mother got weak and so sickly
  She was forced to quit sewing at last;
This made our lot very much harder,
  For the most I could earn at the store
Was so small that I found it not easy
  To keep the grim wolf from the door.

My Adonis could see I was troubled,
  And offered to give me right there
Enough money to keep us from starving,
  He said he had plenty to spare.
In such straits how could I gainsay him?
  I thought him an angel of grace!
In my worship I gave him my treasure,
  So would you had you been in my place.

But to shorten a lengthy sad story,
  Half a year had gone over my head
When poor mother discovered my folly—
  Next day she lay on her death bed.
For years I had been her sole worship,
  Her idol, her joy and her pride.
And with tears coursing down her poor wrinkles,
  She kissed me and blessed me, and died.

Left alone, I implored the protection
  Of him who had brought me to shame,
But he suddenly fled from our city
  With the brand of a criminal's name.
But if he'd return to my bosom,
  Though he hadn't a penny to give,
I'd forget all the sorrow he caused me,
  And love him as long as I live.

But there's no chance of his ever coming,
  Or any one leading the way
To make me a good honest woman,
  So a girl of the town I must stay.
In this world I know I'm a lost one,
  But the last judgment day you may see
That the Saviour who cheered the Magdalene
  Will put in a good word for me.

—*Unknown*

★　★　★　★

ROCK ME TO SLEEP

by Elizabeth Akers Allen

Backward, turn backward, O time, in your flight;
Make me a child again, just for tonight!
Mother, come back from that echoless shore;
Take me again in your heart as of yore—
Kiss from my forehead the furrows of care,
Smooth the few silver threads out of my hair,
Over my slumbers your loving watch keep—
Rock me to sleep, mother—rock me to sleep!

Backward, turn backward, O tide of the years!
I am so weary of toil and of tears—
Toil without recompense, tears all in vain—
Take them and give me my childhood again!
I have grown weary of dust and decay—
Weary of flinging my soul-wealth away—
Weary of sowing for others to reap—
Rock me to sleep, mother—rock me to sleep!

Tired of the hollow, the base, the untrue,
Mother, O mother, my heart calls for you!
Many a summer the grass has grown green,
Blossomed and faded—our faces between—
Yet with strong yearning and passionate pain,
Long I tonight for your presence again;
Come from the silence so long and so deep—
Rock me to sleep, mother—rock me to sleep!

Come, let your brown hair, just lighted with
       gold,
Fall on your shoulders again as of old—
Let it drop over my forehead tonight,
Shading my faint eyes away from the light!
For, with its sunny-edged shadows once more,
Haply will throng all the visions of yore;
Lovingly, softly, its bright billows sweep—
Rock me to sleep, mother—rock me to sleep!

Mother, dear mother! the years have been long
Since last I listened to your lullaby song;
Sing, then, and unto my soul it shall seem
Womanhood's years have been only a dream;
Clasped to your heart in a loving embrace,
With your light lashes just sweeping my face,
Never hereafter to wake or to weep—
Rock me to sleep, mother—rock me to sleep!

SAM BASS
And How
His Career Was Short

Sam Bass was born in Indiana, it was his native
    home,
And at the age of seventeen young Sam began
    to roam.
Sam first came out to Texas a cowboy for to
    be—
A kinder-hearted fellow you seldom ever see.

Sam used to deal in race stock, one called the
    Denton mare,
He matched her in scrub races, and took her to
    the Fair.
Sam used to coin the money and spent it just as
    free,
He always drank good whisky wherever he might
    be.

Sam left the Collins' ranch in the merry month
    of May
With a herd of Texas cattle the Black Hills for
    to see,
Sold out in Custer City and then got on a
    spree—
A harder set of cowboys you seldom ever see.

On their way back to Texas they robbed the
    U.P. train,
And then split up in couples and started out
    again.
Joe Collins and his partner were overtaken
    soon,
With all their hard-earned money they had to
    meet their doom.

Sam made it back to Texas all right side up with
 care;
Rode into the town of Denton with all his
 friends to share.
Sam's life was short in Texas; three robberies
 did he do,
He robbed all the passengers, mail, and express
 cars too.

Sam had four companions—four bold and daring
 lads—
They were Richardson, Jackson, Joe Collins,
 and Old Dad;
Four more bold and daring cowboys the rangers
 never knew,
They whipped the Texas Rangers and ran the
 boys in blue.

Sam had another companion, called Arkansas
 for short,
Was shot by a Texas ranger by the name of
 Thomas Floyd;
Oh, Tom is a big six-footer, and thinks he's
 mighty fly,
But I can tell you his racket—he's a deadbeat on
 the sly.

Jim Murphy was arrested, and then released on
 bail;
He jumped his bond at Tyler and then took the
 train for Terrell;
But Mayor Jones had posted Jim and that was
 all a stall,
'Twas only a plan to capture Sam before the
 coming fall.

Sam met his fate at Round Rock, July the
    twenty-first,
They pierced poor Sam with rifle balls and
    emptied out his purse.
Poor Sam he is a corpse and six foot under clay,
And Jackson's in the bushes, trying to get away.

Jim had borrowed Sam's good gold and didn't
    want to pay,
The only shot he saw was to give poor Sam
    away.
He sold out Sam and Barnes and left their
    friends to mourn—
Oh, what a scorching Jim will get when Gabriel
    blows his horn.

Perhaps he's got to heaven, there's none of us
    can say,
But if I'm right in my surmise he's gone the
    other way.

—Unknown

★   ★   ★   ★

THE FLAT RIVER GIRL

Come all you fine young fellows with hearts so
    fond and true,
Never believe in women for you are lost if you
    do;
But if you ever see one with a long, brown chest-
    nut curl,
Just think of Jack Haggerty and his Flat River
    girl.

212

Her form was like the dove, so slender and so
    neat,
Her long, brown chestnut curl hung to her tiny
    feet,
Her voice it was like music or the murmur of
    the breeze
As she whispered that she loved me as we strolled
    among the trees.

She was the blacksmith's daughter from the Flat
    River side,
And I always had intended for to make her my
    bride;
But one day on the river a letter I received;
She said that from her promise she craved to be
    relieved.

To her mother, Jane Tucker, I lay all the blame,
She caused her to leave me and to blacken my
    name;
I counted her my darling, what a lady for a wife!
When I think of her treachery it nearly takes my
    life.

Come all you fine young fellows with hearts so
    warm and true,
Never believe in a woman; you are lost if you
    do;
But if you ever see one with a long, brown chest-
    nut curl,
Just think of Jack Haggerty and his Flat River
    girl!

—Unknown

CAPTAIN JINKS

I am Captain Jinks of the Horse Marines,
I often live beyond my means,
I sport young ladies in their 'teens,
   To cut a swell in the army.
I teach the ladies how to dance,
How to dance, how to dance,
I teach the ladies how to dance,
   For I'm their pet in the army.
Spoken: Ha! Ha! Ah!

CHORUS

I'm Captain Jinks of the Horse Marines,
I give my horse good corn and beans;
Of course it's quite beyond my means,
   Though a captain in the army.

I joined the corps when twenty-one,
Of course I thought it capital fun,
When the enemy came then off I run,
   I wasn't cut out for the army.
When I left home mamma she cried,
Mamma she cried, mamma she cried,
   "He ain't cut out for the army."
Spoken: No, she thought I was too young, but
   then,
   I said, "Ah! Mamma." (CHORUS)

The first day I went out to drill,
The bugle-sound made me quite ill,
At the balance step my hat it fell,
   And that wouldn't do for the army.
The officers they all did shout,
They all cried out, they all did shout,
The officers they all did shout,
   "Oh, that's the curse of the army."
Spoken: Of course my hat *did* fall off, but, ah!
   Nevertheless, (CHORUS)

My tailor's bills came in so fast,
Forced me one day to leave at last,
And ladies, too, no more did cast
  Sheep's eyes at me in the army.
My creditors at me did shout,
At me did shout, at me did shout,
My creditors at me did shout,
  "Why, kick him out of the army."
Spoken: I said, "Ah, gentlemen, ah! Kick *me* out
    of the army? Perhaps you are not aware
    that . . . (CHORUS)

—*Unknown*

* * * *

OUT WHERE THE WEST BEGINS

by Arthur Chapman

John Chapman, noted drama critic of the New York
News, sends me this note on his father's famous verse: "It
was in 1912. My father, Arthur Chapman, was conducting
a column on the Denver Republican, and in Buffalo there
was a convention of state governors. Dad saw a news item
about the governors' having got into an argument over
just where the West began. So he wrote 'Out Where the
West Begins.' To my father it was just another piece for
the column; but to the linotype operator who set it from
the original typewritten copy it seemed better than average,
and he asked if he could keep the original. Dad said, 'Sure.'
I don't know who the printer was."

Out where the handclasp's a little stronger,
Out where the smile dwells a little longer,
  That's where the West begins;
Out where the sun is a little brighter,
Where the snows that fall are a trifle whiter,
Where the bonds of home are a wee bit tighter,
  That's where the West begins.

215

Out where the skies are a trifle bluer,
Out where friendship's a little truer,
    That's where the West begins;
Out where a fresher breeze is blowing,
Where there's laughter in every streamlet flowing,
Where there's more of reaping and less of sowing,
    That's where the West begins.

Out where the world is in the making,
Where fewer hearts in despair are aching,
    That's where the West begins;
Where there's more of singing and less of sighing,
Where there's more of giving and less of buying,
And a man makes friends without half trying,
    That's where the West begins.

★ ★ ★ ★

DO YOU FEAR THE
FORCE OF THE WIND?

by Hamlin Garland

Do you fear the force of the wind,
    The slash of the rain?
Go face them and fight them,
    Be savage again.
Go hungry and cold like a wolf,
    Go wade like the crane:
The palms of the hands will thicken,
    The skin of your cheek will tan,
You'll grow ragged and weary and swarthy,
    But you will walk like a man!

OLD DAN TUCKER

by

Dan D. Emmet

I come to town de udder night,
I hear de noise den saw de sight,
De watchmen dey were runnin' roun,
Cryin' Old Dan Tucker's come to town,
     Git out ob de way! (BANJO)
     Git out ob de way! (BANJO)
Git out ob de way old Dan Tucker,
Your too late to come to your supper.

Tucker is a nice old man,
He used to ride our darby ram,
He sent him whizzin' down de hill,
If he hadn't got up—he'd laid dar still.
     Git out ob de way! *etc.*

Sheep an de hog walkin' in de pastur
Sheep sez "hog can't y'e go a little faster?
Hush! hush honey! hear de wolf howlin!
Ah, ah, de lawd—old bull dog growlin,"
     Git out ob de way! *etc.*

Jaybird in de martin's nest,
To sabe he soul he got no rest,
Ole Tucker run in de fox's den
Out come de young ones—nine or ten.
     Git out ob de way! *etc.*

Tucker on de wood pile—can't count 'lebben,
Put in a fedder bed—him gwine to hebben,
His nose so flat, his face so full,
De top ob his head like a bog ob wool.
      Git out ob de way! *etc.*
Tucker went round hickory steeple,
Dar he met some colored people.
Some was black and some was blacker,
Some was de color ob brown tobacur.
      Git out ob de way! *etc.*

High-hold on de holler tree.
He poke his bill in for to see,
De lizzard cotch 'im by de snout,
He call old Tucker to pull 'im out.
      Git out ob de way! *etc.*

Tucker he had cash a plenty,
Dressed to death—his old trunck empty,
To kiss de gals he thot was useless,
'Cept he kissed wid a sway-back-looseness.
      Git out ob de way! *etc.*

Here's my razor in good order,
Magnum bonum—jis hab bought 'er,
Sheep shell de oats, old Tucker shell de corn
I'll shabe you all when de water gets warm.
      Git out ob de way! *etc.*

I went to meetin' de udder day,
To hear old Tucker preach and pray,
Dey all got drunk, but me alone,
I make old Tucker—walk jaw-bone,
      Git out ob de way! (BANJO)
      Git out ob de way! (BANJO)
Git out ob de way you harden'd sinner,
Your too late to come to your dinner.

THE HOUSE BY THE SIDE OF THE ROAD

by Sam Walter Foss

There are hermit souls that live withdrawn
In the place of their self-content;
There are souls like stars, that dwell apart,
In a fellowless firmament;
There are pioneer souls that blaze their paths
Where highways never ran—
But let me live by the side of the road
And be a friend to man.

Let me live in a house by the side of the road,
Where the race of men go by—
The men who are good and the men who are
   bad,
As good and as bad as I.
I would not sit in the scorner's seat,
Or hurl the cynic's ban—
Let me live in a house by the side of the road
And be a friend to man.

I see from my house by the side of the road,
By the side of the highway of life,
The men who press with the ardor of hope,
The men who are faint with the strife.
But I turn not away from their smiles nor their
   tears,
Both parts of an infinite plan—
Let me live in a house by the side of the road
And be a friend to man.

I know there are brook-gladdened meadows
    ahead,
And mountains of wearisome height;
That the road passes on through the long after-
    noon
And stretches away to the night.
But still I rejoice when the travelers rejoice,
And weep with the strangers that moan,
Nor live in my house by the side of the road
Like a man who dwells alone.

Let me live in my house by the side of the road,
It's here the race of men go by—
They are good, they are bad, they are weak, they
    are strong,
Wise, foolish—so am I;
Then why should I sit in the scorner's seat,
Or hurl the cynic's ban?
Let me live in my house by the side of the road
And be a friend to man.

* * * *

MY MARYLAND

by James Ryder Randall

The despot's heel is on thy shore,
    Maryland!
His torch is at thy temple door,
    Maryland!
Avenge the patriotic gore
That flecked the streets of Baltimore,
And be the battle-queen of yore,
    Maryland, my Maryland!

Hark to an exiled son's appeal,
    Maryland!
My Mother State, to thee I kneel,
    Maryland!
For life and death, for woe and weal,
Thy peerless chivalry reveal,
And gird thy beauteous limbs with steel,
    Maryland, my Maryland!

Thou wilt not cower in the dust,
    Maryland!
Thy beaming sword shall never rust,
    Maryland!
Remember Carroll's sacred trust,
Remember Howard's warlike thrust,
And all thy slumberers with the just,
    Maryland, my Maryland!

Come! 'tis the red dawn of the day,
    Maryland!
Come with thy panoplied array,
    Maryland!
With Ringgold's spirit for the fray,
With Watson's blood at Monterey,
With fearless Lowe and dashing May,
    Maryland, my Maryland!

Dear Mother, burst the tyrant's chain,
    Maryland!
Virginia should not call in vain,
    Maryland!
She meets her sisters on the plain,—
"*Sic semper!*" 'tis the proud refrain
That baffles minions back amain,
    Maryland!
Arise in majesty again,
    Maryland, my Maryland!

Come! for thy shield is bright and strong,
  Maryland!
Come! for thy dalliance does thee wrong,
  Maryland!
Come to thine own heroic throng
Stalking with Liberty along,
And chant thy dauntless slogan-song,
  Maryland, my Maryland!

I see the blush upon thy cheek,
  Maryland!
For thou wast ever bravely meek,
  Maryland!
But lo! there surges forth a shriek,
From hill to hill, from creek to creek,
Potomac calls to Chesapeake,
  Maryland, my Maryland!

Thou wilt not yield the Vandal toll,
  Maryland!
Thou wilt not crook to his control,
  Maryland!
Better the fire upon thee roll,
Better the shot, the blade, the bowl,
Than crucifixion of the soul,
  Maryland, my Maryland!

I hear the distant thunder hum,
  Maryland!
The Old Line's bugle, fife and drum,
  Maryland!
She is not dead, nor deaf, nor dumb;
Huzza! she spurns the Northern scum!
She breathes! She burns! She'll come! She'll
  come!
    Maryland, my Maryland!

WHY ARE YOU WEEPING, SISTER?

Why are you weeping, sister? Why are you
    sitting alone?
I'm old and gray and I've lost my way,
All my to-morrows were yesterday,
I traded them off for a wanton's pay,
I bartered my graces for silks and laces,
My heart I sold for a pot of gold,
Now I'm old.

Why did you do it, sister? Why did you sell
    your soul?
I was foolish and fair and my form was rare,
I longed for life's baubles and did not care,
When we know not the price to be paid we dare,
I listened when vanity lied to me
And I ate the fruit of the bitter tree,
Now I'm old.

Why are you lonely, sister? Where have your
    friends all gone?
Friends I have none for I went the road
Where women must harvest what men have
    sowed,
And they never come back when the field is
    mowed,
They gave the lee of the cup to me,
But I was blinded and would not see,
Now I'm old.

Where are your lovers, sister? Where are your
    lovers now?
My lovers were many but all have run,
I betrayed and deceived them every one,
And they lived to learn what I had done,
A poisoned draught from my lips they quaffed,
But I who knew it was poisoned—laughed,
Now I'm old.

Will they not help you, sister, in the name of
    your common sin?
There is no debt for my lovers bought,
They paid my price for the things I brought,
I made the terms so they owe me naught,
I have no hold for 'twas I who sold,
One offered his heart but mine was cold,
Now I'm old.

Where is that lover, sister? He will come when
    he knows your need.
I broke his hope and I stained his pride,
I dragged him down in the undertide,
Alone and forsaken by me he died,
The blood that he shed is on my head,
For all the while I know that he bled,
Now I'm old.

Is there no mercy, sister, for the wanton whose
    course is spent?
When a woman is lovely the world will fawn,
But not when her beauty and grace are gone,
When her face is seamed and her limbs are
    drawn,
I've had my day and I've had my play,
In my winter of loneliness I must pay,
Now I'm old.

What of the morrow, sister? How shall the
    morrow be?
I must feed to the end upon remorse,
I must falter alone in my self-made course,
I must stagger along with my self-made cross,
For I bartered my graces for silks and laces,
My heart I sold for a pot of gold,
Now I'm old.

—Unknown

★   ★   ★   ★

OH! SUSANNA

by Stephen Foster

I come from Alabama
  Wid my banjo on my knee,
I'm g'wan to Lousiana,
  My true love for to see;
It rained all night the day I left,
  The weather it was dry,
The sun so hot I froze to death;
  Susanna, don't you cry.

Oh! Susanna,
  Don't you cry for me,
I come from Alabama
  Wid my banjo on my knee.

I jumped aboard de telegraph
  And trabbled down de ribber,
De lectric fluid magnified,
  And killed five hundred nigger;

De bullgine bust, de horse run off,
  I really thought I'd die;
I shut my eyes to hold my breath,
  Susanna, don't you cry.   (CHORUS)

I had a dream de udder night,
  When eberyting was still;
I thought I saw Susanna,
  A coming down de hill;
De buckwheat-cake was in her mouth,
  De tear was in her eye,
Says I, I'm coming from de South,
  Susanna, don't you cry.   (CHORUS)

Oh! when I gets to New Orleans
  I'll look all round and round,
And when I find Susanna
  I'll fall right on de ground;
But if I do not find her,
  Dis darkey'll surely die,
And when I'm dead and buried,
  Susanna, don't you cry. (CHORUS)

THE CUMBERLAND

by Herman Melville

Some names there are of telling sound,
  Whose vowelled syllables free
Are pledge that they shall ever live renowned;
  Such seems to be
A Frigate's name (by present glory spanned)—
  The Cumberland.
            Sounding name as e'er was sung,
            Flowing, rolling on the tongue—
            Cumberland! Cumberland!

She warred and sunk. There's no denying
  That she was ended—quelled;
And yet her flag above her fate is flying,
  As when it swelled
Unswallowed by the swallowing sea: so grand—
  The Cumberland.
            Goodly name as e'er was sung,
            Roundly rolling on the tongue—
            Cumberland! Cumberland!

What need to tell how she was fought—
  The sinking flaming gun—
The gunner leaping out the port—
  Washed back, undone!
Her dead unconquerably manned
  The Cumberland.
            Noble name as e'er was sung,
            Slowly roll it on the tongue—
            Cumberland! Cumberland!

227

Long as hearts shall share the flame
   Which burned in that brave crew,
Her fame shall live—outlive the victor's name;
   For this is due.
Your flag and flag-staff shall in story stand—
   Cumberland!
        Sounding name as e'er was sung,
        Long they'll roll it on the tongue—
        Cumberland! Cumberland!

★   ★   ★   ★

LEGS

Legs to the right of us,
Legs to the left of us,
Legs in front of us,
   How they display them!
On they go trippingly,
Dainty and skippingly,
Frost that bites nippingly
   Does not dismay them.
Straight legs and bandy ones,
Bum legs and dandy ones,
Awkward and handy ones,
   Flirt with the breezes.
Round legs and flatter ones,
Thin legs and fatter ones,
Especially the latter ones,
   Showing their kneeses.
Straight and distorted ones,
Mates and ill-sorted ones,
Home and imported ones—
   Ain't we got fun?

                        —Unknown

WHEN A FELLOW
BEGINS TO GET BALD

As age creeps upon us we try to stay young
  And as frisky as long as we can,
And show to the world by both action and
    tongue
We yet are a mighty good man.
We laugh at gray hairs as no token of age,
  But look in the mirror appalled
As we find we are facing that worrying stage
  When a fellow begins to get bald.

It fastens a look of deep care in the eyes,
  It anchors a dread in the soul,
For here is a feature we cannot disguise,
  A skating rink up on the poll.
The fiend of anxiety tortures the brain,
  Our taste for enjoyment is palled,
Our pleasure is tinged with a color of pain
  When a fellow begins to get bald.

We blow in our money for tonics and creams,
  We try all the lotions in sight,
But every preventive we plaster on seems
  To hasten the hair in its flight.
We wear out our shoes on the specialist's stairs,
  Experts into council are called,
But every day adds to the burden of cares
  When a fellow begins to get bald.

We sit away back at the naughty display
    Of tights in the high-kicking show,
Through fear that our friends may inhumanly
        say,
    We've hit the old bald-headed row.
At night our once pleasant, delectable dreams
    By visions of wings are enthralled,
When waking, the brain with keen misery teems
    When a fellow begins to get bald.

Whenever we meet lady friends on the street
    We blush when uplifting our hat,
And though they may smile with a greeting most
        sweet
    We know they have got us down pat.
We seem to care little when to our reward,
    In the realms of the blest we are called,
For half of the pleasure of living seems floored,
    When a fellow begins to get bald.

—*Unknown*

* * * *

THERE WAS A LITTLE GIRL

by Henry Wadsworth Longfellow

There was a little girl, she had a little curl
    Right in the middle of her forehead;
And when she was good, she was very, very good,
    And when she was bad, she was horrid.

230

THE DEATH OF JESSE JAMES

The spelling of the elder James boy's first name on the old copy I unearthed was "Jessie," which I accepted as authentic; this might have brought the wrath of the whole state of Missouri on my unsuspecting head. But a distinguished Missouri author and, incidentally, an old friend of the James family corrected me. "Jesse" it is.

It was on a Wednesday night, the moon was
    shining bright,
  They robbed the Glendale train.
And the people they did say, for many miles
    away,
  'Twas the outlaws Frank and Jesse James.

Jesse had a wife to mourn all her life,
  The children they were brave.
'Twas a dirty little coward shot Mister Howard,
  And laid Jesse James in his grave.

It was Robert Ford, the dirty little coward,
  I wonder how he does feel,
For he ate of Jesse's bread and he slept in Jesse's
    bed,
  Then he laid Jesse James in his grave.

It was his brother Frank that robbed the Gal-
    latin bank,
  And carried the money from the town.
It was in this very place that they had a little
    race,
  For they shot Captain Sheets to the ground.

They went to the crossing not very far from
    there,
  And there they did the same;
And the agent on his knees he delivered up the
    keys
  To the outlaws Frank and Jesse James.

It was on a Saturday night, Jesse was at home
  Talking to his family brave,
When the thief and the coward, little Robert
    Ford
  Laid Jesse James in his grave.

How people held their breath when they heard
    of Jesse's death,
  And wondered how he ever came to die.
'Twas one of the gang, dirty Robert Ford,
  That shot Jesse James on the sly.

Jesse went to his rest with his hand on his breast.
  The devil will be upon his knee.
He was born one day in the county of Clay,
  And came from a solitary race.

—*Unknown*

THE END OF THE TRAIL

This is a tale of the wanderlust trail—
Of a man with his back to the wall—
So all you flip guys who think you are wise
Take heed and avert your downfall.
Now I'm a wise egg, who can lie, steal or beg,
And I've traveled this whole world around;
I've been East and been West, I'm there with
    the best
When it comes to covering the ground.

I've handled a pick along side of a spick,
Laying steel on the D. R. & G.,
And I've done the heavy on the New Orleans'
    levee,
Sailed on a whaler to sea.
I've juggled a tray in a New York cafe,
Hopped bells in a hotel in Chi';
Carried a pack along the B. & O. track,
Caught red ball freights on the fly.

I've lain in my cell and suffered like hell
For the want of a big shot of dope,
And I've begged in despair to be sent to the
    chair,
Or bumped off at the end of a rope.
I've ranted and raved for the drug that I craved,
To soothe my ragged, raw nerve;
I've prayed without hope to the Goddess of
    Dope
Whose every bidding I'd serve.

All my life I've roamed, without friend or home,
Up and down the old cinder trail,
And now it seems all I have is my dreams
Of days that were spent out of jail
So heed to this tale of the wanderlust trail,
You can see how it ended for me.
Stay right in the sticks with the rest of the
    hicks—
That's a convict's warning from me!

—Unknown

★ ★ ★ ★

HANDSOME HARRY

Handsome Harry, handsome Harry Thomas
    He was sued, yes, sued for breach of promise.
He took Mary walking thro' the dell
    And Mary promised not to tell.
Mary went right home and told her mother.
    Ma told Pa, and Pa told her brother.
Brother told the preacher, and
    The preacher tolled the wedding bells.

Never take a walk with Mary,
    Never take a walk with Sue,
Never take a walk with Maud or Carrie,
    That's the kind of girl you'll have to marry.
When you want to go out walking,
    Strolling thro' the shady dell,
Always take a girl named Daisy,
    'Cause daisies don't tell.

—Unknown

THE STORMY WINDS
DO BLOW

'Twas Friday morn we all set sail,
  And we were not far from land,
When all at once we espied a mermaid
   With a comb and a glass in her hand,
    In her hand,
   With a comb and a glass in her hand.

CHORUS

The stormy winds do blow, blow, blow,
  And the raging seas how they flow;
While we poor sailors are climbing to the top,
   And the landsmen lying down below,
    Down below,
   And the landsmen lying down below.

Then up spoke the captain of that gallant ship,
  And a right gallant captain was he:
"I've a father and mother in me own native land,
   Who'll be watching and waiting for me,
    For me,
   Who'll be watching and waiting for me."

Then up spoke the bo'sun of that gallant ship,
  And a right gallant bo'sun was he:
"I've a wife and a child in me own native land,
   Who'll be watching and waiting for me,
    For me,
   Who'll be watching and waiting for me."

Then three times around went our gallant ship,
   And three times around went she;
And the last time around she turned up her rump,
   And sank to the bottom of the sea,
     Of the sea,
And sank to the bottom of the sea.

—Unknown

*   *   *   *

DRIED APPLE PIES

I loath, abhor, detest, despise,
Abominate dried apple pies.
I like good bread, I like good meat,
Or anything that's fit to eat;
But of all the poor grub beneath the skies,
The poorest is dried apple pies.
Give me the toothache, or sore eye,
But don't give me dried apple pies.
The farmer takes his gnarliest fruit,
'Tis wormy, bitter, and hard, to boot;
He leaves the hulls to make us cough,
And don't take half the peeling off.
Then on a dirty cord 'tis strung
And in a garret window hung,
And there it serves as roost for flies,
Until it's made up into pies.
Tread on my corns, or tell me lies,
But don't pass me dried apple pies.

—Unknown

MY MOTHER
WAS A LADY

by Edward B. Marks

A Denver newspaperman and myself were watching a
performance of an old melodrama at the American Music
Hall there and enjoying it thoroughly. Between the acts
the girls who served drinks sang this ballad of long ago.
While we did not actually cry in our beer, we both felt an
upsurge of chivalry in our hearts.

Two drummers sat at dinner, in a grand hotel
    one day,
While dining they were chatting in a jolly sort
    of way,
And when a pretty waitress brought them a tray
    of food,
They spoke to her familiarly in a manner rather
    rude;

At first she did not notice them or make the least
    reply,
But one remark was passed that brought the tear
    drops to her eye,
And facing her tormentor, with cheeks now
    burning red,
She looked a perfect picture as appealingly she
    said:

"My mother was a lady—like yours you will
    allow,
And you may have a sister, who needs protec-
    tion now,
I've come to this great city to find a brother
    dear,
And you wouldn't dare insult me, Sir, if Jack
    were only here."

It's true one touch of nature, it makes the whole
    world kin,
And ev'ry word she uttered seemed to touch
    their hearts within,
They sat there stunned and silent, until one
    cried in shame,
"Forgive me, Miss! I meant no harm, pray tell
    me what's your name?"
She told him and he cried again, "I know your
    brother, too,
Why, we've been friends for many years and he
    often speaks of you,
He'll be glad to see you, and if you'll only wed,
I'll take you to him as my wife, for I love you
    since you said: (CHORUS)

THE

LITTLE RED GOD

Here is one paralleling Kipling's "If." It was written
some time before the latter.

Here's a little red song to the god of guts,
Who dwells in palaces, brothels, huts;
The little Red God with the craw of grit;
The god who never learned how to quit;
He is neither a fool with a frozen smile,
Or sad old toad in a cask of bile;
He can dance with a shoe-nail in his heel
And never a sign of his pain reveal;
He came hold a mob with an empty gun
And turn a tragedy into fun;
Kill a man in a flash, a breath,
Or snatch a friend from the claws of death;
Swallow the pill of assured defeat
And plan attack in his slow retreat;
Spin the wheel till the numbers dance
And bite his thumb at the god of Chance;
Drink straight water with whisky-soaks,
Or call for liquor with temperance folks;
Tearless stand at the graven stone,
Yet weep in the silence of night, alone;
Worship a sweet, white virgin's glove,
Or teach a courtesan how to love;
Dare the dullness of fireside bliss,
Or stake his soul for a wanton's kiss;
Blind his soul to a woman's eyes
When she says she loves and he knows she lies;

Shovel dung in the city mart
To earn a crust for his chosen art;
Build where the builders all have failed,
And sail the seas that no man has sailed;
Run a tunnel or dam a stream,
Or damn the men who finance the dream;
Tell a pal what his work is worth,
Though he lose his last, best friend on earth;
Lend the critical monkey-elf
A razor—hoping he'll kill himself;
Wear the garments he likes to wear,
Never dreaming that people stare;
Go to church if his conscience wills,
Or find his own—in the far, blue hills.

He is kind and gentle, or harsh and gruff;
He is tender as love—or he's rawhide tough;
A rough-necked rider in spurs and chaps,
Or well-groomed son of the town—perhaps;
And this is the little Red God I sing,
Who cares not a wallop for anything
That walks or gallops, that crawls or struts,
No matter how clothed—if it hasn't guts.

—Unknown

★   ★   ★   ★

"Go ask Papa," the maiden said,
But the young man knew her papa was dead,
And he knew the life her papa had led,
So she knew that he knew what she meant when
    she said,
        "Go ask Papa."

—Unknown

THE CRY OF THE DREAMER

by John Boyle O'Reilly

Young John Boyle O'Reilly was sentenced to a prison
term in Australia by the British courts, but he escaped
and came to Boston, where he became editor of "The
Pilot" and a poet of distinction. Dr. Oliver Wendell
Holmes was his friend, and O'Reilly was of the group that
bought a horse and buggy for the aging Walt Whitman.
Many can share the feelings he expressed in "The Cry of
the Dreamer."

I am tired of planning and toiling
   In the crowded hives of men,
Heart-weary of building and spoiling,
   And spoiling and building again,
And I long for the dear old river,
   Where I dreamed my youth away;
For a dreamer lives forever,
   And a toiler dies in a day.

I am sick of the showy seeming,
   Of life that is half a lie;
Of the faces lined with scheming
   In the throng that hurries by;
From the sleepless thought's endeavor
   I would go where the children play;
For a dreamer lives forever,
   And a thinker dies in a day.

I can feel no pride, but pity,
   For the burdens the rich endure;
There is nothing sweet in the city
   But the patient lives of the poor.
Oh, the little hands too skillful,
   And the child-mind choked with weeds!
The daughter's heart grown willful
   And the father's heart that bleeds!

No! no! from the street's rude bustle,
   From trophies of mart and stage,
I would fly to the wood's low rustle
   And the meadows' kindly page.
Let me dream as of old by the river,
   And be loved for my dreams alway;
For a dreamer lives forever,
   And the toiler dies in a day.

★ ★ ★ ★

THE LETTER

The postman has come and he's brought me a
     letter;
   The handwriting's shakey—it's merely a scrawl;
But still, to my notion, no penmanship's better;
   It's from an old lady who's feeble and small—
A mother who loves me, a mother who's yearning
   To have me start homeward while she is still
     there;
Whose thoughts and whose hopes to her boy are
     e'er turning—
   The boy for whom nightly she murmurs a
     pray'r.
It tells me her roses are just a bit tardy—
   The rain has been awful, this year, mother
     writes;

It tells me that Rover, the dog, always hardy,
Has lately been hurt in some terrible fights.
To you it's inane, gentle reader, I know it;
To me it's a mighty sweet little affair.
Someday I intend to just pack up and go it,
   And visit the home place while mother's still
     there.
                        —*Unknown*

FIVE KERNELS OF CORN

by Hezekiah Butterworth

April, 1622

'Twas the year of the famine in Plymouth of old,
The ice and the snow from the thatched roofs
    had rolled;
Through the warm purple skies steered the geese
    o'er the seas,
And the woodpeckers tapped in the clocks of the
    trees;
And the boughs on the slopes to the south winds
    lay bare,
And dreaming of summer, the buds swelled in
    the air.
The pale Pilgrims welcomed each reddening
    morn;
There were left but for rations Five Kernels of
    Corn.
  Five Kernels of Corn!
  Five Kernels of Corn!
But to Bradford a feast were Five Kernels of
    Corn!

"Five Kernels of Corn! Five Kernels of Corn!
Ye people, be glad for Five Kernels of Corn!"
So Bradford cried out on bleak Burial Hill,
And the thin women stood in their doors, white
    and still.
"Lo, the harbor of Plymouth rolls bright in the
    spring,
The maples grow red, and wood robins sing,
The west wind is blowing, and fading the snow,
And the pleasant pines sing, and the arbutuses
    blow.
  Five Kernels of Corn!
  Five Kernels of Corn!
To each one be given Five Kernels of Corn!"

O Bradford of Austerfield haste on thy way.
The west winds are bowing o'er Provincetown
   Bay,
The white avens bloom, but the pine domes are
   chill,
And new graves have furrowed Precisioners'
   Hill!
"Give thanks, all ye people, the warm skies have
   come,
The hilltops are sunny, and green grows the
   holm,
And the trumpets of wind, and the white March
   is gone,
And ye still have left you Five Kernels of Corn.
   Five Kernels of Corn!
   Five Kernels of Corn!
Ye have for Thanksgiving Five Kernels of Corn!

"The raven's gift eat and be humble and pray,
A new light is breaking, and Truth leads your
   way;
One taper a thousand shall kindle: rejoice
That to you has been given the wilderness
   voice!"
O Bradford of Austerfield, daring the wave,
And safe through the sounding blasts leading
   the brave,
Of deeds such as thine was the free nation born,
And the festal world sings the "Five Kernels of
   Corn!"
   Five Kernels of Corn!
   Five Kernels of Corn!
The nation gives thanks for Five Kernels of
   Corn!
To the Thanksgiving Feast bring Five Kernels
   of Corn!

THE LURE OF THE TROPICS

You've decided to come to the tropics,
Heard all that you had to do
Was to sit in the shade of a cocoanut glade,
While the dollars rolled in to you.

You got that stuff down at the bureau,
Have you got your statistics straight?
Well, hear what it did to another kid
Before you decided your fate.

You don't go down with a sharp, hard fall,
You just sort of shuffle along,
And lighten your lad of the moral code
Till you don't know right from wrong.

I started in to be honest,
With everything on the square;
But the man can't fool with the Golden Rule
In a crowd that won't play fair.

'Twas a case of riding a crooked race,
Or being an "also ran";
My only hope was to sneak and dope
The horse of the other man.

I pulled a deal in Guayaquil,
In an Inca silver mine;
And before they found it was salted ground,
I was safe in the Argentine.

But the thing that'll double-bar my soul,
When it flaps at heaven's doors,
Was peddling booze to the Santa Cruz
And Winchester forty-fours.

Made unafraid by my hellish aid,
The drink-crazed brutes came down
And left a blazing, quivering mass
Of a flourishing border town.

I then took charge of a smuggler's barge,
Down the coast from Yucatan;
But she went to hell off Christobel
One night, in a hurricane.

I got to shore on a broken oar,
In the filthy, shrieking dark,
While the other two of the good ship's crew
Were converted into shark.

From a sun-baked cliff I flagged a skiff,
With a salt-soaked pair of jeans;
Then worked my way—for I couldn't pay—
On a fruiter to New Orleans.

It's a kind of habit, the tropics—
It gets you worse than rum;
You'll get away and you swear you'll stay,
But they call, and back you come.

Six short months went by before
I was back there on the job,
Running a war in Salvador
With a barefoot, black-faced mob.

A mob that made me general,
Leading a "grand" revolt,
And my only friend from start to end
Was a punishing army Colt.

I might have become their president,
A prosperous man of means;
But a gunboat came and spoiled my game,
With a hundred and ten marines.

So I awoke from my dream, dead broke,
And drifted from bad to worse,
And sank as low as a man can go
Who walks with an empty purse.

But stars, they say, appear by day,
When you are down in the deep, dark pit;
My lucky star found me that way
When I was about to quit.

Alone on a hot, flea-ridden cot,
I was down with the yellowjack;
Alone in the bush and damned near dead—
She found me and brought me back.

In her eyes shone lights of empires gone,
For hers was the blood of kings—
When she spoke, her voice inspired high
    thoughts
And dreams of nobler things.

We were spliced in a Yankee meeting house
In the land of your Uncle Sam;
And I drew my pay from the U.S.A.
For I worked on the Gatun dam.

Then the devil sent his right-hand man,
I might have suspected he would;
And he took her life with a long, thin knife,
Because she was pure and good.

Within me died hope, honor, and pride,
And all but a primitive will
To hound him down on his blood-red trail,
And find, and kill, and kill!

O'er chicle camps and logwoods swamps,
I hunted him many a moon;
Then found my man in a long pit pan,
At the edge of a blue lagoon.

The chase was o'er at the farther shore,
It ended a two-year quest;
And I left him there with an empty stare,
And a knife stuck in his chest.

You see those marks upon my arm?
You wonder what they mean?
Those marks were left by fingers deft
Of my trained nurse—Miss Morphine.

You may say that habit's no worse than rum?
It's possible, too, you are right;
But at least it drives away the things
That come and stare at night.

There's a homestead down in an old Maine
    town,
And there's lilacs 'round the gate,
And the night winds whisper, "it might have
    been,"
But the truth has come too late.

For whenever you play, whatever the way,
For stakes that are large or small,
The law of the tropics gathers it in,
And the dealer gets it all.

—*Unknown*

COME HOME, FATHER

by
Henry
Clay
Work

How many sorely tempted footsteps did these tragic lines lead safely past the saloon door and on to the happy home? Ah, but if they paused, sniffing the aromatic odors from the swinging doors, then the Lord pity the poor hungry children. (See back cover.)

Father, dear Father, come home with me now,
  The clock in the steeple strikes one;
You said you were coming right home from the
    shop,
  As soon as your day's work was done;
Our fire has gone out, our house is all dark,
  And Mother's been watching since tea,
With poor brother Benny so sick in her arms,
  And no one home to help her but me.
Come home! Come home! Come home!
  Please, Father, *dear* Father, come home.

Hear the sweet voice of the child,
Which the night winds repeat as they roam;
Oh, who could resist this most plaintive of
  prayers,
"Please, Father, dear Father, come home."

Father, dear Father, come home with me now,
  The clock in the steeple strikes two;
The night has grown colder, and Benny is worse,
  But he has been calling for you;
Indeed he is worse, Ma says he will die,
  Perhaps before morning shall dawn;
And this is the message she sent me to bring:
  "Come quickly, or he will be gone." (CHORUS)

Father, dear Father, come home with me now,
  The clock in the steeple strikes three;
The house is so lonely, the hours are so long,
  For poor weeping Mother and me;
Yes, we are alone; poor Benny is dead,
  And gone with the angels of light;
And these were the very last words that he said:
  "I want to kiss Papa good night." (CHORUS)

EVOLUTION

by Langdon Smith

When you were a Tadpole and I was a Fish
   In the Paleozoic time,
And side by side on the ebbing tide
   We sprawled through the ooze and slime,
Or skittered with many a caudal flip
   Through the depths of the Cambrian fen,
My heart was rife with the joy of life,
   For I loved you even then.

Mindless we lived and mindless we loved
   And mindless at last we died;
And deep in the rift of the Caradoc drift
   We slumbered side by side.
The world turned on in the lathe of time,
   The hot lands heaved amain,
Till we caught our breath from the womb of
     death
   And crept into light again.

We were amphibians, scaled and tailed,
   And drab as a dead man's hand;
We coiled at ease 'neath the dripping trees
   Or trailed through the mud and sand.
Croaking and blind, with our three-clawed feet
   Writing a language dumb,
With never a spark in the empty dark
   To hint at a life to come.

251

Yet happy we lived and happy we loved,
  And happy we died once more;
Our forms were rolled in the clinging mold
  Of a Neocomian shore.
The eons came and the eons fled
  And the sleep that wrapped us fast
Was riven away in a newer day
  And the night of death was past.

Then light and swift through the jungle trees
  We swung in our airy flights,
Or breathed in the balms of the fronded palms
  In the hush of the moonless nights;
And, oh! what beautiful years were these
  When our hearts clung each to each;
When life was filled and our senses thrilled
  In the first faint dawn of speech.

Thus life by life and love by love
  We passed through the cycles strange,
And breath by breath and death by death
  We followed the chain of change,
Till there came a time in the law of life
  When over the nursing sod
The shadows broke and the soul awoke
  In a strange, dim dream of God.

I was thewed like an Auroch bull
  And tusked like the great cave bear;
And you, my sweet, from head to feet
  Were gowned in your glorious hair.
Deep in the gloom of a fireless cave,
  When the night fell o'er the plain
And the moon hung red o'er the river bed
  We mumbled the bones of the slain.

I flaked a flint to a cutting edge
  And shaped it with brutish craft;
I broke a shank from the woodland lank
  And fitted it, head and haft;
Then I hid me close to the reedy tarn,
  Where the mammoth came to drink;
Through the brawn and bone I drove the stone
  And slew him upon the brink.

Loud I howled through the moonlit wastes,
  Loud answered our kith and kin;
From west and east to the crimson feast
  The clan came tramping in.
O'er joint and gristle and padded hoof
  We fought and clawed and tore,
And cheek by jowl with many a growl
  We talked the marvel o'er.

I carved that fight on a reindeer bone
  With rude and hairy hand;
I pictured his fall on the cavern wall
  That men might understand.
For we lived by blood and the right of might
  Ere human laws were drawn,
And the age of sin did not begin
  Till our brutal tusks were gone.

And that was a million years ago
  In a time that no man knows;
Yet here tonight in the mellow light
  We sit at Delmonico's.
Your eyes are deep as the Devon springs,
  Your hair is dark as jet,
Your years are few, your life is new,
  Your soul untried, and yet—

Our trail is on the Kimmeridge clay
  And the scarp of the Purbeck flags;
We have left our bones in the Bagshot stones
  And deep in the Coralline crags;
Our love is old, our lives are old,
  And death shall come amain;
Should it come today, what man may say
  We shall not live again?

God wrought our souls from the Tremadoc beds
  And furnished them wings to fly;
He sowed our spawn in the world's dim dawn,
  And I know that it shall not die,
Though cities have sprung above the graves
  Where the crook-boned men made war
And the oxwain creaks o'er the buried caves
  Where the mummied mammoths are.

Then as we linger at luncheon here
  O'er many a dainty dish,
Let us drink anew to the time when you
  Were a Tadpole and I was a Fish.

Here's to the girl who is mine—all mine.
She drinks and she bets, and she smokes ciga-
    rettes,
And sometimes, I am told, she goes out and
    forgets
—that she's mine—all mine!

—Unknown

THE MEN

OF THE ALAMO

by James Jeffrey Roche

What names came to my mind the day long ago I stood in the Alamo! Bowie, Crockett, Barrett Travis, brave men all, going to their deaths against overwhelming odds. Here is a chapter that will adorn the pages of American history forever.

To Houston at Gonzalés town, ride, Ranger, for
    your life,
Nor stop to say good-bye to-day to home, or
    child, or wife;
But pass the word from ranch to ranch, to every
    Texan sword,
That fifty hundred Mexicans have crossed the
    Nueces ford,
With Castrillon and perjured Cos, Sesmá and
    Almonte,
And Santa Anna ravenous for vengeance and for
    prey!
They smite the land with fire and sword; the
    grass shall never grow
Where northward sweeps that locust herd on
    San Antonio!

Now who will bar the foeman's path, to gain a
    breathing space,
Till Houston and his scattered men shall meet
    him face to face?
Who holds his life as less than naught when
    home and honor call,
And counts the guerdon full and fair for liberty
    to fall?
Oh, who but Barrett Travis, the bravest of them
    all!
With seven score of riflemen to play the rancher's
    game,
And feed a counter-fire to halt the sweeping
    prairie flame;
For Bowie of the broken blade is there to cheer
    them on,
With Evans of Concepcion, who conquered Cas-
    trillon,
And o'er their heads the Lone Star flag defiant
    floats on high,
And no man thinks of yielding, and no man
    fears to die.

But ere the siege is held a week a cry is heard
    without,
A clash of arms, a rifle peal, the Ranger's ringing
    shout,
And two-and-thirty beardless boys have bravely
    hewed their way
To die with Travis if they must, to conquer if
    they may.
Was ever valor held so cheap in Glory's mart
    before
In all the days of chivalry, in all the deeds of
    war?
But once again the foemen gaze in wonderment
    and fear

To see a stranger break their lines and hear the
    Texans cheer.
God! how they cheered to welcome him, those
    spent and starving men!
For Davy Crockett by their side was worth an
    army then.
The wounded ones forgot their wounds; the
    dying drew a breath
To hail the king of border men, then turned to
    laugh at death.
For all knew Davy Crockett, blithe and generous
    as bold,
And strong and rugged as the quartz that hides
    its heart of gold.
His simple creed for word or deed true as the
    bullet sped,
And rung the target straight: "Be sure you're
    right, then go ahead!"

And were they right who fought the fight for
    Texas by his side?
They questioned not; they faltered not; they
    only fought and died.
Who hath an enemy like these, God's mercy slay
    him straight!—
A thousand Mexicans lay dead outside the con-
    vent gate,
And half a thousand more must die before the
    fortress falls,
And still the tide of war beats high around the
    leaguered walls.
At last the bloody breach is won; the weakened
    lines give way;
The wolves are swarming in the court; the lions
    stand at bay.
The leader meets them at the breach, and wins
    the soldier's prize;

A foeman's bosom sheathes his sword when gallant Travis dies.
Now let the victor feast at will until his crest be
    red—
We may not know what raptures fill the vulture
    with the dead.
Let Santa Anna's valiant sword right bravely
    hew and hack
The senseless corse; its hands are cold; they will
    not strike him back.
Let Bowie die, but 'ware the hand that wields
    his deadly knife;
Four went to slay and one comes back, so dear
    he sells his life.
And last of all let Crockett fall, too proud to sue
    for grace,
So grand in death the butcher dared not look
    upon his face.

But far on San Jacinto's field the Texan toils are
    set,
And Alamo's dread memory the Texan steel shall
    whet.
And Fame shall tell their deeds who fell till all
    the years be run.
"Thermopylae left one alive—the Alamo left
    none."

* * * *

THE

FATAL

WEDDING

by

W. H. Windom

The wedding bells were ringing on a moonlight
    winter's night,
And the church was decorated, all within was
    gay and bright.
A mother with her baby came and saw the lights
    aglow,
She thought how these same bells chimed out for
    her three years ago;
"I'd like to be admitted, sir," she told the sexton
    old,
"Just for the sake of baby to protect him from
    the cold."
He told her that the wedding there was for the
    rich and grand,
And with the eager watching crowd outside she'd
    have to stand.

CHORUS

While the wedding bells were ringing, while the
    bride and groom were there
Marching up the aisle together, while the organ
    pealed an air;

259

Telling tales of fond affection, vowing never
    more to part—
Just another fatal wedding, just another broken
    heart.

She begged the sexton once again to let her pass
    inside.
"For baby's sake you may step in," the gray
    haired man replied.
"If anyone knows reason why this couple should
    not wed,
Speak now, or hold your peace forever," soon the
    preacher said.
"I must object," the woman cried in voice so
    meek and mild,
"That bridegroom is my husband, sir, and this
    our little child."
"What proof have you?" the preacher asked.
    "My infant," she replied.
She raised the babe, then knelt to pray—the
    little one had died.

The parents of the bride then took the outcast
    by the arm,
"We'll care for you through life," they said, "you
    saved our child from harm."
The parents, bride and outcast wife then quick-
    ly drove away;
The bridegroom died by his own hand before
    the break of day.
No wedding feast was spread that night; two
    graves were dug next day,
One for the darling baby, and in one the father
    lay.
The story, it has oft been told by firesides warm
    and bright,
Of parents, bride and outcast wife, and a fatal
    wedding night.

IN THE
BAGGAGE COACH AHEAD

by Gussie Davis

On a dark, stormy night as the train rattled on,
  All the passengers had gone to bed,

Except one young man with babe in his arms,
  Who sat there with bowed down head;

The innocent one began crying just then,
  As though its poor heart it would break,

When an angry man said: "Make that child stop
  its noise,
  For it is keeping all of us awake."

"Put it out," said another, "don't keep it in here,
  We have paid for our berths and want rest,"

But never a word said the man with the child,
  As he fondled it close to his breast.

"Where is its mother? Go take it to her,"
  This a lady then softly said.

"I wish that I could," was the man's sad reply,
  "But she's dead in the coach ahead!"

CHORUS

While the train rolled onward, a husband sat
  in tears,

Thinking of the happiness of just a few short
  years,

261

For baby's face brings pictures of a cherished
    hope that's dead,

But baby's cries can't waken her, in the baggage
    coach ahead.

Every eye filled with tears, when his story he told,
    Of a wife that was faithful and true:

He told how he'd saved up his earnings for years,
    Just to build up a home for two;

How when heaven had sent them this sweet little
    babe,
    Their young happy lives were blessed,

His heart seemed to break when he mentioned
    her name,
    And in tears tried to tell them the rest,

Every woman arose to assist with the child,
    There were mothers and wives on that train;

And soon was the little one sleeping in peace,
    With no thought of sorrow or pain.

Next morn at the station he bade all goodbye,
    "God bless you," he softly said;

Each one had a story to tell in their homes
    Of the baggage coach ahead.

Check these first lines with your memory:

264

Index of Titles and Authors